ENDORSEME[ ]

"In this book, enthusiastic global de [...]
together to extract innovative and [...]
lessons from their common, personal [...]
mative experiences to develop communities through emp[...]
erment and respect. These lessons are applicable worldwide,
by those who want to reduce human suffering using an equity
approach."

*- **Dr. Agnes Binagwaho**, Vice Chancellor of University of Global
Health Equity, Butare, Rwanda*

"With candid stories about their personal experiences and
exercises for the reader at the end of each chapter, Igoye, Karrel,
and Van Leeuwen illuminate the values of the Global Livingston Institute's "Listen. Think. Act." framework. Beyond its
profound relevance to community development, 'Listen. Think.
Act.: Lessons and Perspectives in Community Development'
provides vital insights for leaders in any field."

*- **Dr. Angela Thieman Dino**, Senior Instructor, University of
Colorado, Boulder*

"For anyone considering or already engaged in community
development work, Agnes, Thomas, and Jamie share practical
and personal experiences that will challenge and inspire you to
think deeply about how to best involve and engage communities on the journey to creating lasting change."

*- **Denis Kibirige**, Legislative Draftsman of the East African
Community*

LISTEN. THINK. ACT.

Lessons and Perspectives in Community Development

Agnes Igoye, Thomas Karrel, and Jamie Van Leeuwen

GLOBAL
LIVINGSTON
INSTITUTE
LISTEN. THINK. ACT:

Listen. Think. Act.
GLI Global Livingston Institute. Listen. Think. Act.
©2021
Denver, Colorado
Lake Bunyonyi, Kabale, Uganda
All rights reserved

ISBN: 978-1-7376-9770-1

Book layout by Jena Skinner

100% of book sales will go to support the community development work of
GLI and the Dream Revival Center in Uganda.

TABLE OF CONTENTS

FOREWARD

This is not your typical textbook. I write this foreword as someone who felt deeply moved while participating in this project as editor of this book. I am not an expert on Uganda, and I have only been to East Africa twice in my life—once to visit a friend shortly after college, and then many years later with the Global Livingston Institute as part of a book project I was working on that was in part about a family from the Democratic Republic of Congo who found refuge in a settlement in Uganda after fleeing conflict. However, my brief encounters with the people that I met during that journey have stayed with me. I remember standing with staff from GLI in long lines at the border crossings, the arduous and bumpy road trip we made together across remote areas as we traveled to the refugee settlement in western Uganda that was sheltering so many people in need of a safe home, and the glimpses I got of life in the big cities in sub-Saharan Africa. I distinctly remember the people we met and the astonishing stories that they shared about the communities where they were living. I have always cared deeply about trying to get to know other people better by listening to the stories they have to tell.

This book brings all of this to life. The authors take you into various communities in East Africa and the United States and provide key perspectives on how we should approach local and international community development work. It is a textbook that will better inform a student seeking to travel to a new country and connect with a non-government organization to try to make the world a better place. But it is also a book for people who are simply interested in building stronger communities at home or abroad, and for people who travel to other places around the planet and wonder what they should do when someone on the street approaches them and asks them to pay their school fees. It is a book that truly inspires anyone who wants to better understand community development and what it means to Listen. Think. Act.

As a storyteller myself, I appreciate the way that this book uses the art of storytelling to teach the reader how to engage in an iterative process of continual improvement while attempting community development. The stories you will find in this book are real and the encounters are genuine. In reading what the authors have to share, you come to learn why it is important sometimes to "just stand there" as opposed to "just do something," as overly hasty action can have unintended consequences. I also believe this book is just getting started and there will be many future iterations to write as we continue to learn and work together as global citizens.

There are many more stories to be told that will continue to guide our various societies on the best way to approach community development work, whether that be in Kalamazoo or Kampala. And there is a lot of community work still to be done. As community development workers, educators, conservationists, and public health leaders, the opportunity to impact change exists all around the globe. While this work requires a sense of urgency, how we all engage in community development work is paramount. The opportunity to do a lot of good exists, but this text reminds us how important it is to pay attention to our approach, and that we can sometimes even make things worse when we think we are making them better!

All that to say, please keep reading. There is a lot to unpack in the pages ahead. I hope that you enjoy the journey this book offers as much as I have enjoyed the journey I have taken with the Global Livingston Institute. By listening and thinking a great deal before we act in concert with others, there is a lot that can be learned along the way.

Helen Thorpe
Journalist and Author
Denver, Colorado

AUTHORS' NOTE

This book is written as "we": a cross-cultural group of three people, united by friendship and a set of shared beliefs and values regarding how to do truly good community development work.

Agnes Igoye is a Ugandan who has devoted her life to issues surrounding human trafficking, migration, and other human rights, and used her voice and powerful personal journey to inspire thousands of people around the globe, ranging from young scholars to national leaders. Thomas Karrel is an American who believes in the transformative powers of cross-cultural exchange and travel as tools for building a better society for all. He specializes in designing interactive and immersive curricula and programs to allow for community conversations to flourish. Jamie Van Leeuwen is an American who has devoted decades of his life to growing community development organizations throughout the United States and the world, sparking partnerships, collaboration, and growth across sectors, and connecting people around the globe.

Throughout the book, we will at times deviate from our collective "we" voice, to allow each author to share personal accounts of lessons that strengthen and bring to life the book's larger themes. We hope you enjoy our collective story as much as WE have enjoyed writing it.

Listen. Think. Act.

PROLOGUE
Connect with Our Community

Who is this book for? The short answer is that we wrote this book for anyone interested in doing good community development work, the tenets and definition of which merit their own discussion that you will find throughout this text.

Who created this book? We are a trio of people from diverse backgrounds who have devoted much of our adult lives to community development work, and who met and began collaborating after participating in efforts to improve our own home communities, both in the United States and in East Africa. We then began to work together to create more authentic partnerships with like-minded people living in those two regions, attempting to reach across the physical divide of the Atlantic Ocean and the cultural divide of colonialism and its aftermath. We will share more about ourselves and our cross-cultural work as we go along.

To get us started, for the purposes of this book, good community development is something that maximizes the collective well-being of a target population and limits suffering from preventable problems. It increases the quality of life of communities with an eye towards equity. What we find compelling is that community leaders, nonprofit professionals, artists, businesspeople, politicians, entrepreneurs, researchers, and educators all engage in community development work every day, without necessarily realizing it. Some do it better than others. It is an art, a trade, a skill, a science. It requires practice and experience to do it well. We wrote this book because, more than ever, the world needs leaders around the globe who can master good community development.

In preparation for writing this book, we reflected on our time as students with a passion for community development, reading textbooks from a wide variety of subjects and disciplines. In turn, we spent time reflecting on our years in the field, and how little our studies and these books truly prepared us for the real work at hand. It is probably not surprising that there are few, if any, textbooks about which we have fond memories, or that we really need to go and read again. Some of them we probably never read all the way through, if we opened them at all. Some of our best textbook memories involved the opportunity to return them to the university bookstore to recover a pittance (relative to what we had paid for them) to spend on a proper celebration marking the end of another semester! It is unlikely you will ever hear anyone say over a hot date or a stimulating dinner party, "I have this really great textbook you should read!" With this book, we are hoping to change that.

Over the course of this book, you will read about our personal experiences doing community development work and about our collaborative efforts through the Global Livingston Institute (GLI), the organization that brought the three of us together. In the spirit of the work we have done through this organization, we have taken a unique approach to writing this book. Our goal was to produce a textbook that would tell a story with a unique voice and engage our readers to reflect on their own values and communities, to help bring these topics to life. Based on our experiences as practitioners, researchers, educators, and humans, we believe that if we tell the story of community development and demonstrate how to truly engage people differently, then we might be able to write a textbook that becomes something more than a chore for students to get through; a textbook that makes the reader actually look forward to what the next chapter has to say; a textbook that might be a topic of discussion and promote dialogue over a family dinner or long road trip. We wanted to produce a textbook that prompts you to start listening and thinking more about the actual practice of good community development, even if you might not agree with everything we say. And when you finish reading this book, we hope that you will ultimately determine how you define "good" community development. Is it the same as the way we define it, or do you see another angle?

This will also not be the most technical book on the planet. If you are interested in anthropology, public health, sociology, economics, policy, public administration, diplomacy, political science, or any of the other fields relevant to doing good community development work, there are plenty of more substantive books out there. This book is our best effort to share real-life stories and applied collective knowledge about the nuanced world of community development that we have seen over decades across the United States, Uganda, and the rest of the world.

Our audience and topic are broad, but we hope to provide clarity in how our world should approach community development work. We hope that with each turn of the page, you think about how you can listen, think, and act to effect positive change in your own community, or wherever your community development work takes you. For the purposes of this textbook, we explore how you get started and what community development looks like from the ground up. We look at how the principles of this work can translate from Denver, Colorado, to Kampala, Uganda, or the other way around. Framed by our own core values at the GLI of Listen. Think. Act., we start with the foundations of good community development, through story-sharing and empathy-building, and then move to exchanging ideas, building relationships, and fostering collaborations. We look at forming strategic partnerships and investing in alliances that are built to last. We showcase both the advantages of approaching your work this way and the inherent challenges of being bold enough to collaborate.

We then bring it all together and look at the secret sauce of community development. Spoiler alert: There is no secret sauce! Good community development work takes time, and we have to roll up our sleeves and dig in. It takes substantial effort, patience, and determination, and sometimes it requires not a second chance or a third chance but a fourth and fifth chance until we get it right. Ultimately, good community development workers should build a solid résumé of failures—otherwise known as learning opportunities—and thus become ever better equipped to more closely approximate success. We constantly remind the reader that once we have started acting, we need to listen and think again to determine if the actions we have put forward are actually working. Community development needs to be measured and evaluated constantly; it is time consuming, frustrating, complicated and at times just plain exhausting. But when done well, community development initiatives truly transform communities and change lives. Worth it!

Throughout the book we are going to feature a series of transformative moments in our own professional journeys. These are experiences that have fundamentally changed the way we think about the world and the way we do our work. Even if we may not have realized it at the time, when we look back, we realize that one conversation we had or one encounter we experienced truly altered how we do our work, and in many cases shaped those shared values and beliefs that we bring to community development.

While we hope to make this more engaging than your average textbook, it is still a textbook. You will have homework. At the end of each chapter, you will assume the role of a community development leader (if you haven't already in real life) and design your own intervention to address a real problem in your community. We call this the "Community Changemaker Challenge"! This exercise was inspired by Stanford University's D School's methodology (Raz, 2018) and informed by curricula from other pioneering organizations such as IDEO (IDEO, 2021), and Tulane University's Phyllis M. Taylor Center for Social Innovation and Design Thinking (Taylor Center, 2021). "Design thinking" is a solutions-based approach to solving real-world problems. When you hear the word "design", you might think this method is more relevant to architects or engineers than to community development professionals, but this approach can be used by almost anyone who wants to rigorously think about, and address, a given problem or challenge. As a practitioner of community development, you too are an architect of change.

You can also expect to encounter thought-provoking questions, or "conversation starters," and additional recommended content after each chapter. This content should inform your own group discussions among colleagues and other community development practitioners. It should also lead to other questions that we haven't asked! For this textbook to be worth your time and investment, you should take it out for a test drive. Ask your friends and family what they think. Reflect on our questions and come up with some of your own. Reflect on the case studies and go back and re-read sections that interest you. These are real people in real situations doing real community development work. Think about the roles they play and what roles you hope to assume in your own work. You might find some incidental career coaching or meet some people whose ideas can be pivotal to your own professional and academic development.

At times, you might also find yourself in disagreement with the position that we take or a community perspective we present. If you are looking for the "silver bullet" or the "quick win" in community development, you should put this text on the shelf or return it to the bookstore and move on to the next one. We do not have it. If it is out there, we would love to read about it.

If you, like us, are ready to embrace complexity and approach this topic with both humility and a spirit of innovation, discovery, and determination, we hope this book will prove useful to you. There are other stories and there are other perspectives out there, and like any good scholar you should assemble all of those into your toolbox to make your own assessment about best practices in community development. The stories you find here are mostly told from the perspectives of people who live and work in the United States and Uganda, people who have seen and experienced many different approaches to this work through nongovernmental, governmental, and private organizations, and continue to succeed and fail in their efforts to improve communities around the globe. There are stories from people who know what good community development looks like and who are actively engaging in the science themselves. These are stories we hope you will recommend or recount to someone you meet who wants to create meaningful change and positive impact in their own respective community but is not sure how. The issues may be different, but we have a feeling that the approaches and the values will be the same.

We also want this book to be a starter for young people to inspire them to change the world by engaging in the best possible community development work regardless of their chosen profession. Whether one is a banker, a surgeon, a lawyer, a teacher, or a social worker, there are ways that all these roles can contribute to good community development. We want our readers to think bigger and think differently about how to take on our world's most complex social issues and we want you to understand that each of these issues is, in fact, solvable.

However, this success only happens when we Listen and Think before we Act. With that, turn the page and begin the journey with us.

"Listen. Think. Act. Community development process diagram."
(Graphic created by Thomas Karrel, GLI, October 2021)

PART I: LISTEN

In Part I, LISTEN, we dive into the field of community development and take you on a journey from the United States to Uganda, featuring key points about the importance of listening in practice. We offer community perspectives to highlight work that transcends national borders. This section stresses the need for us to share our stories, change the false narratives and biases we have about different parts of the world, and aim to build empathy with others. Ultimately, this first section of the book underscores how, when it comes to doing good community development work, we need to listen before we act, and seek to understand before we seek to be understood.

"We all have our different stories that are either negative or positive. Everyone you meet along the way has something that they are going through or have gone through; it is only when you take time to hear that person's story that you can start to understand. Everywhere in the world, people are experiencing challenges; the way they react to these challenges is what defines the outcomes."

- Talona Mandela, Peer Educator, Community Activist, and Photographer

CHAPTER ONE
Reinvent the Narrative:
Sharing Stories and Finding Common Ground

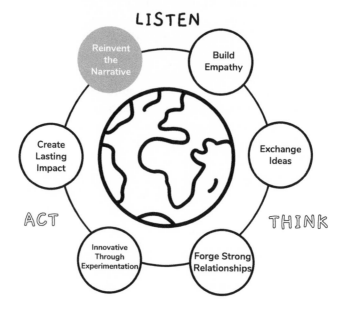

This chapter sets the foundation for doing good community development work and explores the understandable impulse to act quickly when we are confronted with a societal problem that might be urgent and upsetting. This chapter also turns its attention to Africa, a global hub for misdirected community development work, and highlights the challenges that the public, private and nonprofit sectors face when trying to follow "good intentions" with meaningful action. This first chapter sets the tone for the rest of the text as we identify some of the core values that we believe must be in place for any community development work, be it in Denver, Kampala, or anywhere else.

"Don't Just Do Something... Stand There"

The idea that one must "do something" is inculcated in children who grow up in the so-called "West" or "Global North;" in wealthy countries, well-meaning parents, teachers, and community leaders remind children not to stand idle (Vickers, 1977). "There are starving kids out there and they need our help!" *"Don't Just Stand There... Do Something!"* Do something, get it fixed, and then move on. This perspective can create the perception amongst people in the Western world that they know the answers, they know what is needed, and they are not afraid to jump in, insert their values, take charge, and make things better.

Not only did those of us who are from the West learn this in classrooms, but we see it reflected in how our governments respond to issues around the world. There are instances where this approach works. When you knock over a can of soda onto your new iPhone ... don't just stand there, do something. When you see an adorable kitten stuck up in a tree on your way home from school ... don't just stand there, do something. When your sweet grandmother is walking down the drive and slips and falls on the ice ... don't just stand there, do something!

But based on our experiences in community development, we have come to believe that if you are a person from the United States or Europe and you hear about a group of kids in rural Uganda who have no school in their community ... don't just do something ... stand there. When you hear about an urban slum community in Kampala that has no access to electricity ... don't just do something... stand there. When you encounter a young person who needs school fees to go to university ... don't just do something ... stand there.

"Africa Doesn't Need You: A 'Lightning Bolt Moment'," *by Jamie Van Leeuwen*

Back in 2006, I made my way to Lira in Northern Uganda to visit children born of war, hoping to understand what was happening as they were being reintegrated into society after the Lord's Resistance Army (LRA) decimated the region. I stopped at a rural health clinic that I had heard about from a colleague. As is often the case in developing countries, the clinic was run by nuns. One in particular, Sister Jovita, made a lasting impact on me: larger than life, with a contagious laugh and a presence that was cathartic. So here I am at this clinic, where women holding babies are lined up for services and women who have HIV/AIDS and malaria are sick and malnourished seeking care. You would think this would be the most depressing place on the planet, right? It wasn't!

The sisters were all helping and there was a buzz of activity that was palpable. Sister Jovita was showing me around and I was inspired by how much they were doing with what seemed to me like so little. And then she took me into her pharmacy, where the shelves sat bare. We were talking about how she operates the clinic and the extraordinary work that she does with limited resources and I—a 26-year-old gangly, White child of privilege—decided to make my first bold promise to a community in Africa. I told Sister Jovita that I was there to help and was not just going to stand there. We needed to do something.

"Sister Jovita… I will find a way to fill the shelves of your pharmacy with supplies!" She replied with a smile and a laugh. "That would be great Jamie … but if you don't, we will figure it out."

Stop. What? They would figure it out? They did not need my help? This is what I now call my "lightning bolt moment" in international community development. Here was this woman, who every day gets up and figures out how to resourcefully make her way through hundreds of women who need help, without adequate supplies to go around. They have been figuring it out long before some oblivious twenty-something from America showed up at their doorstep, and here I was making a promise to "fix" her clinic.

After Sister Jovita and I got to know each other better, she made clear what she had really been trying to tell me that day:

That would be great if you can provide us with supplies; we could certainly use them. But we have been doing this long before you got here and will continue doing this long after you are gone. We do not need you, but we do want to find ways to work together. That said, I am not going to wait on the corner every day for your skinny White ass to show up and save us. We have work to do!

This was my lightning bolt moment from Uganda, and it echoed similar experiences I had in countries throughout the African continent. Developing and under-resourced communities do not need us, but they do want to work in partnership with us. Don't just do something … stand there, and you will see a genuine interest in collaboration that contradicts our perception that they are waiting for us—or anyone—to show up and "save" them.

———

When we listen to people who grow up in communities throughout Uganda, a nation heavily subjugated by colonial rule, we hear that the power dynamic is sometimes not what it seems. Too often Ugandan communities are on the receiving end of attempts by outsiders to intervene for one externally driven reason after another, and too often local control is thereby compromised. Let us explain.

In a 1968 address to the *Conference on InterAmerican Student Projects (CIASP)* in Cuernavaca, Mexico titled "To Hell with Good Intentions", philosopher and theologian Ivan Illich implored international students not to immediately impose their values on Mexican communities. He blamed lack of training and self-complacency for the many mistakes made in community development efforts staged in Latin America and concluded his remarks with a forceful request that implores community development practitioners and benefactors to listen and think, but not act:

"I am here to entreat you to use your money, your status, and your education to travel in Latin America. Come to look, come to climb [the] mountains, to enjoy [the] flowers. Come to study. But do not come to help" (Illich, 1968).

For the purposes of this text, it is important to realize that "intentions" can mean a lot of things to a lot of people. We see intentions in this context being directly linked to actions. Many people have the intent to do something good in a community, but the question is whether the actions that they employ accomplish what they intend to do.

Illich's strong stance against exporting "good intentions" has merit and his remarks warrant careful consideration and discussion. There is a lot to unpack here, and a lot has happened as it relates to community development over the course of the past 50 years. What is compelling about Illich is that he understood the consequences of uninformed action in developing communities well before his time. The truth that good intentions can still lead to misguided and harmful community work, particularly on the international stage, has gained traction in the past 10-15 years. On top of that, Ivan Illich was a Roman Catholic priest, which makes his harsh public rhetoric against volunteer and missionary work abroad all the more significant. Typically, religious leaders and other theologians are among the biggest proponents of this form of development work.

All that said, the development world has learned a lot since Illich's address. While in some ways his perspectives align with the approach we believe everyone should take to community development, Illich also seems to understate the incredible value of cross-cultural collaboration and partnerships that, when formed in a spirit of equity and exchange, can have positive impacts on both parties involved. We believe that how you help and how you engage in community development matter. There is a significant difference between imposing yourself on, versus engaging with, the communities where you work, regardless of geographic location.

Herein lies our first lesson in community development: listen and think with communities, before you act. Take an approach to community development work that centers around the people you hope to serve and seek to understand before anything else. How you approach and set the foundations of your community development work should be defined by this very principle and is something that we will take a much deeper dive into throughout this book. That said, we start early with this concept as it is quite possibly the most important tenet of community development and the core value of this entire process. It is also arguably one of the most difficult concepts to adopt and practice.

By nature, those of us who come to this field or study this topic do so with the intention of wanting to help or make an impact. We do not want people to suffer unnecessarily, and we want to come to the table with solutions. If someone is hungry, we want to feed them, and if someone is homeless, we want to house them. If we adhere to the tenet that good community development maximizes collective human well-being and limits suffering from preventable problems, then providing food and housing should be part of that. Right? Yes, but it is more complicated than that.

As community development leaders, we should do those things. But how we do them makes a difference and determines whether our solutions will succeed or fail. As Illich might pose, how will your intentions affect the community? We believe this is a fundamental question that every community development worker needs to address as they begin their work and one of the reasons we start with this conversation early on in the book. Illich has a radical approach to how our society should think about action in community development. With the advantage of over five decades of experience, we present an updated take on how to frame action as it relates to community development. Global Health specialist Paul Farmer refers to it as "accompaniment," where [organizations and community members] can work together as equal partners in collaboration to take on some of the most complex problems around the world (Farmer & Weigel, 2013). We will explore this idea in Chapters Three and Four.

This brings us to the next story. As various stakeholders begin to engage each other, a key method is to allow people to share their stories, particularly those who have not often been given this chance or invited to do so. This is invaluable to the community development process. This process of discovery can be transformative. Here is a perspective on the importance of sharing stories that grew out of a women's conference we hosted in southern Uganda.

"The Power of a Ugandan Story," by Agnes Igoye

One year I found myself tucked in a beautiful peninsula on Uganda's deepest lake: Lake Bunyonyi, a.k.a. "the lake of many little birds". We were at the Entusi Resort and Retreat Center, a community-based resort and social enterprise, which was hosting its annual Women's Leadership Retreat. The event served to convene women leaders from all over the United States and East Africa, specifically Uganda, Rwanda, and Kenya. The focus on this day was storytelling, which requires a uniquely safe and open atmosphere. We were a group of women from around the world, all meeting for the first time, to share our stories. Over the years that I have attended this retreat, I have witnessed women open up in this space about stories they have never told anyone in public. This was story sharing, empathy building and active listening exercises like I had never seen before.

One of the things I found most comforting was that after sharing our stories, the women in the audience, without saying a word, would always comfort each other with generous hugs. This kind of deep silence and emotional support speaks volumes.

I have found these experiences on Lake Bunyonyi to be directly applicable when I visit Northern Uganda. They have heightened my ability to be patient and give anyone a chance to truly share their story with me in an open and honest way. In Northern Uganda, I have encountered many women who have suffered gender-based violence in its most extreme forms, telling me their horrific stories; or boys, some who still have unremoved bullets in their bodies, share their stories of abduction and being forced by the dissident group of the Lord's Resistance Army (LRA) to fight as child soldiers and kill their own people. My ability to inspire story sharing with others has been integral to how I ultimately think and act in my community work. This listening phase creates a foundation of respect and honesty that proves invaluable in all my community development projects.

In an experiential learning course for American students that I helped lead in Uganda, we once visited an elderly woman whose husband had been killed during conflict with the LRA, and whose children had been abducted. She was later reunited with two of them. Our visit was the first time she was speaking to anyone about her story. I will never forget it. She was grateful to us for visiting and caring enough to listen to what had happened to her. This interaction came after years of development assistance to Northern Uganda from the Ugandan government and an array of international development organizations had come around. Nobody had ever consulted her or allowed her to properly share her story or her needs before making any development interventions. Internationally renowned documentaries and large-scale development organizations were created out of this conflict, yet this woman made it clear that she and her neighboring communities had not had a voice in those story lines. How can someone create an organization that helps address populations affected by a war, without talking to the people on the ground most affected by that conflict?

I saw in that moment how well-intentioned people often try to intervene prematurely, before they have built the right relationships, or even listened to someone's story.

———

This was about sharing stories, and how invaluable that process is in community development work. In being patient and prioritizing this stage of our process, it is possible to change the narrative around misdirected community development work and ensure that collective efforts for change properly reflect the perspectives of those most impacted by a given issue. This is step one.

Let us quickly follow this story with a perspective from another community, where you will see that the foundations of good community development can be learned not only in post-conflict regions in Northern Uganda. Good community development can happen anywhere: in this case, in Denver, Colorado. Just like in Northern Uganda, it starts with sharing stories, dispelling stereotypes, and defining your intentions. This will set a strong foundation for the community work that you will do, regardless of where you are in the world. This is a story about finding common ground.

———

"Finding Common Ground in Denver," by Jamie Van Leeuwen

I first met John W. Hickenlooper Jr. while he was campaigning for Mayor of Denver in 2002. At that point, I was directing programs at a homeless and runaway youth shelter in Denver called Urban Peak. Later, John would become like family to me. Mentor. Guide. Advisor. Boss. Friend. Colleague. Hero. But back then, he was just one candidate running for office in a crowded field, and I was a young advocate for the homeless.

I followed John during the mayoral campaign, along with a slew of other candidates. He distinguished himself because he was a small business owner and brought ideas that are critical in the public sector, such as, why make enemies if you can make friends? He ingrained in me at a young age the maxim that there is no margin in having enemies. Do everything you can to find common ground with others, even when you disagree. That advice has served me well.

I had no intention of getting involved in the public sector at that time, but all of us working at Urban Peak wanted the candidates to talk about homelessness as we tenaciously advocated for more youth housing and services. As a growing nonprofit, we aspired to become national, maybe international, and we knew that these resources were critical to the street youth we served. We needed more funding and better coordination to move more homeless kids off the streets and into secure housing. And Hickenlooper agreed. He believed that the time was now, and he committed early on that if elected Mayor, he would take on homelessness.

Hickenlooper won. And he took on homelessness. Within months of being elected, he appointed a formidable commission tasked with addressing homelessness. But before the commission created a single unit of housing or changed the way they delivered shelter, mental health, and substance abuse services, they began drafting "Denver's Road Home: A Ten-Year Plan to End Homelessness". They started by listening and thinking with the various stakeholders and learned a lot about how to set the stage to do good community development.

Hickenlooper created a seat at the table for everyone who wanted one and he pushed the commission out of their comfort zone simply due to the variety of people and perspectives seated around the table. If you are going to take on an issue of this complexity and magnitude and make it a priority, you need every sector represented. You need their buy-in, and remember, there is no margin in having enemies. And when they set the table, it looked a lot different than homeless commissions prior. There was a CEO sitting next to a homeless man. There was a police chief sitting next to a homeless services provider. A city council president sitting next to an outreach worker. The head of the Chamber of Commerce sitting next to a homeless mother. And everyone had an equal vote on the commission.

Despite the many perspectives and personalities on the commission, after six months of conversation and contentious debate, Denver had a comprehensive plan to end homelessness. Reflecting on its origins, the plan called for and required the involvement of every sector. And everyone was invited to participate and provide input with the understanding that everything was on the table and up for discussion if people were willing to show up and participate. Thousands of people were engaged. Police officers, elected officials, civil servants, human services and nonprofit professionals, business leaders, neighborhood liaisons, faith communities, funders, homeless youths, and homeless adults. They all had a seat at the table.

Once they were seated at the table, it became apparent that a lack of listening across sectors was an obstacle to achieving a universal guiding purpose. Good community development is about finding common ground and defining your intentions. Finding common ground requires that everyone has a voice, and when people exercise that voice, it will not always be received with empathy or understanding. However, despite some anticipated turbulence, when you work hard and dig deep to find one or two tenets or values that everyone embraces, you can get a lot done. And the relationships you build will help to advance the collective mission.

Finding common ground. It is arguably one of the most critical, and therefore complicated, exercises in community development. We spend an enormous amount of our time as public officials, business leaders and community organizers fighting about topics and issues where we disagree. Often, we choose to dwell on issues where we will most likely never find common ground. It is quite easy to find subjects on which we can disagree. It is much harder to achieve consensus; there is an art to finding those points on which we *can* agree.

Believe it or not, through our early conversations we realized that many key stakeholders in Denver believed that homelessness was an inevitable consequence of modern society. In a sense, they figured that some people would have to be homeless given the complicated nature of economic inequality and urbanization.

With our many differences now on the table, through civil dialogue and sometimes heated exchanges, the members of the Denver homeless commission stayed at the table, and they found something they all agreed on. They found that there was one thing that the most affluent person in the room and the poorest person in the room had in common; something that both the chief of police and the street outreach worker agreed upon. Amid disagreements about the role of law enforcement, public feeding, panhandling, health services, and resource allocation, we found one foundational idea that everyone, I mean everyone, in the room could agree on. Nobody in Denver should have to be homeless.

That was the core idea around which we could build a collective understanding. Through extensive listening together, those harsh doubts about the state of homelessness began to subside. This collective was developing a deeper, more comprehensive understanding of how homelessness affects individuals than ever before.

When asked if there was anyone in the room who thought keeping people homeless was an acceptable solution, there was not a single vote of endorsement. They achieved consensus. And from there, this disparate commission of people, some of whom had never sat at the same table together before, established a bold and coordinated commitment to end homelessness in Denver.

Skipping ahead, this approach to listening and hearing out diverse perspectives from a variety of actors was vital to the success of this work. There was a lot more that went into the design of the plan, but there is a compelling argument that could be made that without listening and thinking first, this bold community development effort would have not achieved the successes it did. Over the next four years, the public, private, and nonprofit sectors would work in coordination with Denver's Road Home to develop over 1,500 new units of housing for the homeless, prevent over 2,232 families from becoming homeless, and find employment for 3,278 people experiencing homelessness. The faith community mentored 564 families out of homelessness, and in partnership with the Mile High United Way, they raised $46.1 million dollars in the first four years of the plan.

––––––

The point of this story is to underscore the importance of creating a seat at the table for all stakeholders, so that everyone in the community is part of the process and can share their stories. In doing so, it is possible to build consensus and find a proper starting point.

Achieving consensus also means taking on misperceptions and establishing a baseline understanding of the issue at hand. To find common ground, everyone who has a seat at the table needs to fully understand the issue at hand. Stereotypes, misperceptions, and value judgements cloud our ability to make informed decisions about our most complex social issues. If we are not operating from a shared baseline set of data, then finding common ground will be difficult, if not impossible. We want to look at this question of how to find common ground in the context of tackling homelessness in urban America, and in attempting community development in East Africa.

Challenging Assumptions and Reimagining Africa

Denver has not cornered the market on finding common ground. We believe it works everywhere and if the core principles were applied more frequently, we might achieve greater success in our actions. How does what happened in Denver translate to what happens in urban or rural settings in countries throughout Africa, or anywhere else in the world? Do these lessons of community development transcend borders?

The short, albeit emphatic, answer is yes. We firmly believe there are core principles of community development that should inform your work, whether you are in Los Angeles or La Paz.

The longer answer is that it is complicated and messy. The Denver's Road Home model, while packed with lessons and mistakes to learn from, cannot simply be applied to addressing homelessness in New York, Nairobi, or New Delhi. Context matters.

Without context, preconceptions can lead us down the wrong road with misguided intentions. Listening and thinking helps us to find that common ground and correct for bad data and information. Our understanding of complex issues, be it homelessness in Denver or poverty in Africa, is often driven by cultural stereotypes and media impressions. The challenge rests in listening and thinking with actual communities to help shape and define our society's intentions, impressions, and responses towards community development work. The common narrative being used needs to be reinvented.

For example, what is the first image that comes to mind when we tell you to think of a person experiencing homelessness in the United States? What do you see and what do they look like? What are their key characteristics? Think about gender, age, appearance, and other observations. Be brutally honest. Stop here and think this through before reading on!

So, what image comes to mind? When we do this exercise with a live audience, everyone is quiet at first until someone blurts out the first characteristic ever so quietly to not offend. But the answers are almost always similar. And then the group piles on. What mental image do you see when you think of a homeless person in the United States?

- Dirty and stinky
- Holding a liquor bottle
- Old
- Beard
- Pushing a shopping cart
- Flying a sign
- Lazy and crazed

These are common and prevailing images that form a perception of millions of Americans when they think of a homeless person. And that perception is destructive when trying to take on homelessness in a meaningful way. This image does not typically motivate a community to want to help, and in most cases, our perceptions about the homeless person reinforce destructive stereotypes ... *"Why would we want to provide services to someone who is lazy?" "Get a job!" "Go to work and quit drinking!"*

Canadian author Malcolm Gladwell teaches us to be more patient and focus on changing the existing and possibly incorrect narrative when we take on complex issues. When he visited John Hickenlooper in Denver to better understand why a new Mayor would be intrepid enough to take on something as intractable as homelessness, Gladwell found that there was a lot more under the surface than he realized. Things are not always as they appear. When he travelled to Reno, Nevada, to listen and think more on the topic, he encountered a man who became known as "Million Dollar Murray." Murray was a man experiencing homelessness, who was a recipient of various public interventions over ten years, ranging from prison to hospitalization. These solutions not only failed to help Murray reclaim a stable life, but cost Nevada taxpayers one million dollars, an incredibly expensive failure on the part of the community (Gladwell, 2006). Homelessness was costly.

When the Denver homeless commission dug deeper and took another look at the issues, the image of that homeless person changed. Often, that lazy, crazy homeless person is a veteran of a foreign war; someone who served our country and returned home to find that their social networks and access to resources did not quite hold up. They are people who would work and pay their taxes and gladly live indoors if they did not have the added barrier of untreated mental health and substance abuse issues. They might not be as old as they look, and they are probably not homeless by choice. They most likely have a family, and they are not where they thought they would be (or wanted to be) when they were a kid and hanging out with their friends on the playground at school. What Gladwell learned is that when you draw conclusions and form perceptions without listening and thinking first, your approach to addressing the issue at hand is misguided from the start. The community development plan you design for a lazy and crazy homeless guy is very different from one you would design for a veteran who is having a difficult time accessing the mental health and substance abuse services needed to maintain housing.

Let us shift our demographics and cross borders. What is the first image that comes to mind when you think of Africa?

- One homogenous region
- Danger and the unknown
- Poverty
- War
- Ebola, Malaria, and other diseases
- Orphanages and foreign volunteers
- People in exotic clothing
- The Lion King

Global literacy tests in the United States demonstrate a profound lack of understanding of the African continent, both in terms of geography and politics. A recent Gallup survey showed that over half of Americans aged 18-24 did not know that Sudan was in Africa (Council on Foreign Relations, 2019). The lack of knowledge about countries that make up the African continent is not limited to U.S citizens today but traces back to damaging generalizations made by former United States Presidents, prominent international development organizations, and university students (Amin, 2016). Lyndon Johnson once labeled Africans as "cannibals," while Richard Nixon ridiculed Black people as being "genetically inferior" to White people. There have been specific examples of United States Peace Corps volunteers recalling "primitive mud huts" all over Africa's varied landscapes, and American college students holding up their image of Africa as a "place of destruction, primitive conditions, and injustice, and where people practice strange religions" (Amin, 2016). Conversations about Africa conjure up subjects like Ebola, rebel soldiers, poverty, famine, corruption, orphanages, and war. Even in 2018, a sitting United States President, Donald Trump, labeled swaths of Africa as part of a group of "shithole" nations during a meeting with United States Senators (Vitali et al., 2018).

Fueled by people who still hold misguided perceptions and stereotypes, every year African countries draw thousands of nongovernmental organizations (NGOs), students, parishes, congregations, volunteers, and missionaries to build, create, and implement on behalf of local communities. In most cases, these groups have the very best of intentions. However, these efforts are often carried out with little-to-no understanding of the communities that are being served, with scant effort toward listening to the community members and learning what they actually want and need. These groups act instead based on their preconceptions of what they *think* is needed, by building schools, shipping laptops, and administering health care.

Due to the lack of a concerted effort to understand the true needs of the communities and rather delivering services based on their own value-based perceptions and judgements, NGOs working across the continent today run the risk of repeating mistakes in Africa that echo earlier travesties. For instance, during the Berlin Conference of 1884-1885, a group of imperialist Western and European leaders carved up Africa into what they thought it should look like, without an informed consideration of tribal and cultural distinctions (Herbst, 2014). A select few European leaders made decisions on behalf of millions of African people about their education, their health care, and their governance, arbitrarily outlining which European nation should preside over each geographical jurisdiction in Africa. Those European leaders single-handedly disintegrated much that was functional about Africa during that conference, under the guise of what they believed would make things better (or at least make them richer). Africa still has not recovered.

> *Additional Learning: The Berlin Conference of 1884–1885 marked a turning point in European imperialism in Africa, commonly known as the "Scramble for Africa." Although the Berlin Conference did not spark European colonization of Africa, it helped formalize the process on a global stage. Shortly following this event, by 1900, European states had claimed almost 90% of Africa's territory (Appiah & Gates, 2010).*

Even today, people often make the classic error of grouping the 54 sovereign nations that make up Africa into one supposedly homogenous and exotic entity. When you ask someone where they are from in the United States, they usually either reference a city or a state. You hear that someone is from "Oregon" or "New York City" or "Omaha, Nebraska." But when traveling somewhere for the summer, you often hear people say that they are going to "Africa." When there is talk about an Ebola crisis you hear people talking about the "Ebola crisis in Africa" with over-generalized warnings like: "Be careful about going to Africa right now, there is an Ebola crisis."

That is like telling someone who is going to Colorado on vacation for a hiking trip that they might want to reconsider their travel plans because there is a hurricane hitting the United States … in Florida. When the 2014 Ebola outbreak in West Africa was making front page news, many tourists, and students we knew cancelled their travel plans to Kampala, Uganda. However, Liberia's capital city of Monrovia, where much of the outbreak was happening, is closer to London than it is to Kampala.

Africa is a continent that covers 11.7 million square miles; to put its size into perspective, note that it could easily contain the entire landmass of the United States, China, and India, with plenty of room to spare (Desjardins, 2020). Africa is the second largest continent in the world, and its population uses between 1,500 and 2,000 unique languages and dialects in addition to English, French, Portuguese, and other European vernaculars (Kästle, 2020). With a population of more than 1 billion people and 3,000 tribes, it is quite telling that we group all these languages, cultures, and ideologies into one "Africa" (Hadithi Africa, 2020). So much is erased when we do.

Few discussions about the continent of Africa begin with talk of its entrepreneurial spirit, its ability to contain and to prevent spread of disease, its unparalleled natural resources, its cultural diversity, or the fact that it is the birthplace of humanity. Africa is a major supplier of popular demands like oil, diamonds, cocoa, coal, and platinum (Custers et al., 2009). Africa's vast amount of vital minerals are essential for the world's software and telecommunication industries, and its booming population has catapulted the continent into becoming the fastest growing mobile telecom market in the world (Signé, 2019). Because of the population's resilience and growing confidence in starting new businesses, as well as many African nations pushing for equality among women and men in the workforce, the continent is quickly becoming a global epicenter of entrepreneurship (Kermeliotis et al., 2014). This is just a tiny slice of what is happening on this rich and complex continent. After taking some time to learn more about Africa's development, it becomes very difficult to hang onto the typical preconceived notions.

As discussed previously, to work on homelessness, you need to understand the affected population and whom you are serving to build the right network of care and coordinated services. The type of housing you create for a newly homeless family with small children is very different from the type of housing you need to create for a veteran who has been homeless for 20 years. And similarly, to work on the African continent, or anywhere else on the globe for that matter, the approach you take with one community is not necessarily the same approach you would take in one that is adjacent. Culture and context matter. To do good community development, regardless of the region or the issue you are taking on, you need to listen first and gradually build an understanding of the culture and geography of the people you are trying to serve. Failure to do so can result in disappointing results and catastrophic mistakes. We will explore the concept of context further in Chapter Three, as we get into idea exchange.

Let us discuss more about how the previous stories manifest in international development. Jamie's first lightning bolt moment highlights an important point in the fundamentals of community development. Earlier we discussed how Malcolm Gladwell sought to better understand the culture and context of the chronically homeless. Consider the following scenario to understand the critical role that uninformed perceptions play in attempts to do community development work across continents.

A Wildly Hypothetical Story with Some Semblance of Truth

A group of Americans from New Orleans, Louisiana, learns about communities in Lira, Uganda, struggling with low test scores, decreasing rates of secondary school attendance, and other barriers to education access. They want to help, and their intentions are good. Don't just stand there, do something ... and they do! They raise money by appealing to the good nature and generous spirit of their friends and family who are delighted to play a role in helping all of those "poor kids in Africa." They travel to Uganda to build a school to fix the multitude of issues lacking in the educational system in Northern Uganda. After the school is built, they leave, with pictures of their brand-new building in hand to share with friends and family and to spread the news of their good deeds through social media posts and emails in which they tell tales of their harrowing humanitarian work. They have done a good thing and helped to support a community, and they are lavished with praise by both the Ugandans they spent the week with and their friends back home.

But what exactly did they do? Illich would want to know if the results of the group's work aligned with their intentions.

- Did they have the impact in Lira that they set out to achieve?
- Did they even have a clear sense of what impact they hoped to achieve?

They acted and achieved their stated goal, which was to build a school. But did they listen and think with the community? Did they ask the right questions? Did they deliver for the community what the community really wanted?

To dissect this hypothetical scenario, let us flip the story around. A group of entrepreneurial and aspiring university students from Lira in Northern Uganda read articles about the education system in New Orleans, Louisiana. They read about race and economic divides related to access to classrooms, infrastructural gaps, and limited resources for teachers. In the 2017-2018 school year, only 29% of New Orleans students performed at or above the Mastery proficiency level, due to economic limitations, lack of transportation, and physical accessibility, among other hindrances (Education Equity Index, 2017). The Ugandan students save up money by crowdfunding, secure their visas, and travel over to the southern United States, equipped with hammers, nails, and plenty of supplies that they brought from home. They arrive at Louis Armstrong International Airport, wearing matching t-shirts ready to help build a school in New Orleans. They are not just standing there … they are doing something! They will stick around for a week and then head home, having addressed, and responded to some of the education barriers in New Orleans, all in the spirit of humanitarianism.

The hypothetical reversal of roles is intended to highlight a larger point, that this kind of humanitarian work happens all the time. The extent of foreign volunteer work in Africa is enormous. In 2011, there were 1.5 million foreign volunteers in sub-Saharan Africa alone, who contributed $117 million worth of services (UN Volunteers, 2011). What were the intentions of these 1.5 million volunteers? Did they achieve what they set out to accomplish? What would those host communities say, if they were being totally honest?

The world spends millions of dollars performing these well-intentioned acts of service in the spirit of generosity. Millions of volunteers go to Africa and achieve set tasks in a given community, often under the assumption that it will make things better based on what they judge people's needs to be. Or perhaps these volunteers are simply trusting someone else's judgment of what local communities' needs are. They assume that their professor, church leader, or organizational supervisor knows what the local needs are, and they do not think to prioritize the listening step of the work. As we will mention many times, community development is a very iterative process, and anyone getting involved with communities needs to be involved in some form of listening and thinking, before acting.

Failure to listen yields damaging results, like outdated textbooks being shipped to teach students about genetic engineering or to inform them of the latest public policy approaches of the Clinton Administration; textbooks that were written before the existence of social media, decades before any of the new readers were even born. Old t-shirts, socks, jeans, and even bras are sent abroad to make sure those less fortunate have something to wear. Old cell phones that do not work are sent with the good intention that someone in an electronics shop in Kampala will repair them and make them work again, when in fact, the devices end up in a landfill, polluting the land and water supply.

In 2015-16, Nigeria alone received 71,000 tons of used electrical electronic equipment, imported primarily from the European Union, China, and the United States (Baldé, 2017). Out of the 71,000 tons of electronic waste, 19% was non-functional and likely contained high levels of mercury, including refrigerators, air conditioners, and televisions (Baldé, 2017). Subsequently, proper recycling and management of this "e-waste" in Nigeria involved the use of illicit labor, including pregnant women and minors, with little or no protective gear (Baldé, 2017). The generous aim of passing down our old electronics to provide a used cell phone to someone who doesn't have one turned into an opportunity to exploit and harm "developing" countries. The Western world often does this without even realizing it. In fact, it is primarily done with very good intentions.

Clothing donations are equally problematic and are linked to long-term structural change for recipient countries. Kenya's textile industry began declining in the 1980s, when the World Bank and other entities scaled up second-hand clothing pipelines to the local economy (Kubania, 2015). To be more specific, Kenya experienced a massive uptake in demand for used clothing from Western nations, contributing to a 96% decline in local textile industry jobs from around 500,000 in the 1980s to about 20,000 in 2015 (Kubania, 2015). Why would you buy textiles locally when rich Western nations are shipping them in for free?

In this case, a large influx of foreign donations caused a restructuring in Kenya's domestic clothing economy, creating a dependency on secondhand imports. Kenya's government, following in the footsteps of Rwanda, is now trying to ban the importation of used clothes to save and reinvigorate its textile industry. However, this new ban could now harm thousands of Kenyans who make a living in the used clothing industry (Kubania, 2015). Even worse, when the East African Community (EAC) pushed for a ban of secondhand clothing from Western nations to promote local production, neo-colonial instincts in the United States kicked into full gear as notable American politicians claimed that this would be a violation of the African Growth Opportunity Act (AGOA), which provides eligible sub-Saharan African countries with duty-free access to the United States market for thousands of products (Kubania, 2015).

The West has created a lucrative industry out of collecting used clothes for "poor people in developing countries" and shipping them to many African countries in bulk. The local markets are flooded with t-shirts advertising the best tequila bar in South Padre Island, Texas, or a high school baseball team in Seattle, Washington. Then politicians argue that a ban by the EAC could harm jobs and revenue in the United States.

Working from the assumption that the United States has resources that could help support African countries does not mean that we should impose our ideas on the communities where we work. Understanding the economics and taking the time to assess the impact of what seems like the right thing to do makes a huge difference. Don't just do something ... stand there. Cultivate your ability to understand your surroundings at a deeper level. Donating your cell phone or used clothes to someone may not actually help. In fact, they might not *need* your used clothes or cell phone.

Adding to the confusion and complexity, experiences on the micro level might obscure trends and effects on the macro level. As people from wealthy nations travel to communities in the developing world with a generous spirit, they are often greeted by local villagers and youth who contradict what we are talking about here. They want the visitor's cell phone and will gladly take any unwanted clothes. Yet even these well-intended "actions," in aggregate, can be unintentionally destructive to communities.

These are the times when it is most important to stand there and listen and think. What are your intentions and do your proposed actions accomplish what you hope to achieve?

Intention: Would you like us to build you a school?
Reality: We will not be able to pay for a teacher, and we will only be there for one week. We are not architects or engineers. If anything goes wrong with the building, you will probably have to figure it out.

Intention: Would you like my old cell phone?
Reality: It is five years old and in disrepair. You will be excited about it until you realize that it doesn't hold a charge. Even if you wanted to repair it or could find someone who knew how, you do not have the money to do so. It will soon pollute a local waterway and endanger the food system.

Intention: Would you like some of my clothes?
Reality: They are not necessarily your size and the reason I am not wearing

them is that they are falling apart and have holes in them. They will not last long but I do not need them anymore. They might help put one or more of your neighbors out of a job.

The underlying dynamics created by these intentions to "do good" and immediately act can be damaging and harmful to local communities. We are not suggesting that new school buildings are unimportant, either in Lira or New Orleans. And clothes and laptops are some of the fundamental accessories that most humans consider indispensable for successful adults to function in the workplace and maintain a decent quality of life. We all need schools. We all need laptops. And most of us need clothes! Yet it is in the flawed delivery of such ostensibly desirable goods that we can really mess up.

What the Western world misses in our overly hasty community development efforts and overlooks with our good intentions unchecked by real understanding is the process that leads us to know whether a new school building is necessary. New Orleans does have a need for new buildings, but the district itself—as embodied by its community's elected leaders—must decide if there are funds available and if a new building is the best use of resources given the myriad issues they are facing at the time. They might decide that instead of spending money on a new school, they would like to spend the money on 10 new teachers to reduce class sizes. They listen and think and come up with courses of action that respond to the actual needs of their district. If local leaders prefer to do this in the United States, then wouldn't it make sense to engage in the same thoughtful decision-making process in other parts of the world? Does Lira really need a new school with all those empty buildings that are visible around the community; or do they instead need solar electricity and a teacher who can train other teachers in the region?

The foundation of good community development, especially for the purposes of this introductory chapter, is the idea that such efforts need to be driven and informed by the community being served. To achieve best results, we should let go of the tendency to approach situations in other communities and other cultures with the idea of solving them the way that we think they should be solved. We must check our cultural biases at the door, take the time to understand the community we hope to connect with, and stand there. We should work toward fostering empathy (Chapter Two), exchanging ideas (Chapter Three), and building relationships (Chapter Four).

Good listening is the key to all of this. There is a well-known Ugandan community leader who captures this point well:

"To bring change to any community, one needs to understand the ways and customs within. This is only possible if one is willing to listen to the small whispers, the small voices that most ignore. You can only align the future goals of a community after all voices have been heard."
– Humphrey Nabimanya, Founder and Team Leader, Reach a Hand Uganda

The people who live in the community where you are working are the best equipped to solve their own problems. They have been there longer than you, they will be there long after you, they understand the cultural context better than you, and they know what they want. A good start to community development work in any situation is to ask the community: "What is it that you want? What role can our organization/group play, if any, to help you get there?" It is crucial to not only factor in the organization's intentions, but the intentions of everyone in that community. What does the community want out of the relationship and what are their intentions?

This conversation can happen in many ways, particularly when skilled specialists are coming into a community to address a very specific issue. For example, a dentist might come in to fix cavities, or a civil engineer might come in to design a locally commissioned foot bridge. In these instances involving industry specialists, the outside stakeholder may not be approaching the entire community to assess general, interdisciplinary development needs; instead, they are bringing a specific service and determining which individuals have the highest need. While dentistry and civil engineering are more standardized disciplines, these situations still provide numerous challenges, as aligning specialists with local community intentions is tricky. We have heard one project example where local kitchen "helpers" were given electric cookstoves, and for understandable reasons, the community welcomed those cookstoves. Why not, right? But new cookstoves were not actually a priority intention for that community. When the project team returned, many of the cookstoves were not in use, and some had been dismantled so that the parts could be used for various other purposes. These stories are unfortunately quite common.

Social issues are not simple and good community development work is messy. The challenges that people face can be profoundly complicated, and any community problem comes with its own baggage: regional or global history, economic dynamics, local cultural context, and more. There is no one-size-fits-all solution when it comes to community development. Keep in mind, if it were easy, everybody would have probably figured it out a long time ago! This work becomes particularly complex when the organizations or "experts" developing interventions are not directly part of a target community. Often, there are racial, cultural, economic, and international barriers between the target community and the outside organization. As we later explore, resource development plays a critical role here. A multitude of complications in community development stem from the daylight between a sound, sustainable program and a one-off program that disappears as soon as the funding does. Good community development requires that we turn the mirror inward even as we endeavor to look outward. With culture and context in mind, there are some other big questions that the community development practitioner and scholar need to sufficiently answer in building the foundations of their work:

- What are the community's desired outcomes?
- How will those outcomes be achieved?
- How will those outcomes be observed or measured?
- Are the outcomes sustainable?
- Is the community driving these intentions, or are you?

We will talk about how to measure these outcomes in Chapter Five, but for now, don't just do something ... stand there.

Summing Up

This chapter was intended to get you thinking about the foundations of community development and the varied contexts in which resulting dynamics play out. The idea is to get you to push the pause button on solving the world's problems, change the limited narrative that often surrounds community development, and first define and understand those challenges with input from the very people who face them. This chapter is not intended to paralyze you into inaction, but to implore you to think more deeply about the consequences of the actions you want to take and the cultural biases and misperceptions that you may bring to the table. There are excellent examples of community development where the community is empowered, and the outcomes are promising and sustainable. But generally, such outcomes involve extensive relationship building prior to action, as we will discuss in Chapters Two and Four.

Trust us, success lies ahead! We did not create these chapters to simply dissuade all those reading from progressing deeper into their community development work. The opportunities to do good community development are endless, and this textbook is designed to motivate you to engage and leverage those opportunities in the right way, regardless of where you do your work.

Many nonprofits and community-based organizations act without listening and thinking first. They arrive somewhere and impart their values and ideas and resources, informed by their own cultural biases. This ultimately repeats the many mistakes of the past. But if you have read this far, you are forewarned about the dangers of overly hasty action and committed to the idea of a more thoughtful approach.

As we lay our foundation to doing good community development, we urge you to push back on the Western world's tendency to act before listening and thinking. Instead of immediately doing something, let us stand there, define intentions together, and work in concert to understand communities and what they actually need. Let us listen and think, before we act.

Chapter One "Community Changemaker" Challenge: IDENTIFY

As discussed in the Prologue, we have some homework for you; we call this the "Community Changemaker Challenge!" Throughout this book we are asking you to become an architect for community development. We want you to design your own intervention to address an "area of interest" that points towards real problems that your community faces. For this first step, you have three tasks:

- Identify your community. This can be defined by geographical location, age, race/culture, socioeconomic status, belief system, or any other relevant parameters. A couple examples are "Vietnamese adolescent population in New Orleans East", or "elderly Christian women in Gashora, Rwanda."
- Identify an area of interest that you want to address in your community. Start big. The interest area will likely be multifaceted and complex, and not something that is easily fixed. Some examples may be childhood education, access to capital, urban development, or mental health.
- Identify your specific user(s). Through this design challenge, "users" are the people that are directly affected by the interest area, and subsequent community development issues. Try to be specific. If you are in New Orleans, your user should (probably) not be the entire population of New Orleans, but maybe someone from a certain neighborhood, age group, gender, ethnicity, or even a specific church or school. If this is something you face personally, feel free to design with your family or close friends as the users.

Think of it in these terms: if you identify "mental health" as your area of interest, the outcome of this challenge is to redesign your user's experience related to mental health issues! Think about a specific experience that you or someone close to you has had. Choose a specific experience that is tangible and real and preferably something that you feel passionate about addressing. Think differently; think big. Here we go!

CHAPTER ONE CONVERSATION STARTERS

- What is your narrative? What is a story that is foundational to your identity?
- How do you share your personal story with others?
- Who normally listens to you? How do you know that they are listening?
- Who do you wish would listen to you? How do you know that they are not listening?
- Which environments do you find best suited to good story sharing?
- How do you find common ground amongst your community? With your friends and family? How about with strangers?
- What does "community development" mean to you?
- What approaches in community development work well and what challenges still exist?
- How would you define "public service" and how does it differ from community development?
- What assumptions and biases might you have about different cultures and communities? How can you begin to address those biases?
- Think about a time when you or someone you know tried to help but made things worse. What happened? How is that relevant to the lessons in Chapter One?
- Research an example of a community development project either domestically or internationally that did not work. Why? What went wrong? Dissect the project's trajectory and use it as an example as you work through this text.

CHAPTER ONE ADDITIONAL RECOMMENDED CONTENT

- Adegoke, Y. C. (2017, June 26). *UN: Half of world's population growth is likely to occur in Africa.* CNN.
- Adichie, C. N. (2009, October 7). *The danger of a single story.* TED Talks.
- Gladwell, M. (2006, February 13). *Million-Dollar Murray: Why problems like homelessness may be easier to solve than to manage.* The New Yorker.
- Herbst, J. (2014). *States and Power in Africa: Comparative Lessons in Authority and Control - Second Edition (Princeton Studies in International History and Politics, 149)* (2nd ed.). Princeton University Press.
- Igoye, A. (2014, January 4). *Did you ever fall and never get up?* Agnes Igoye at TEDxNakaseroWomen 2013. YouTube.
- Illich, I. (1968, April 20). *To Hell with Good Intentions.* Conference on InterAmerican Student Projects (CIASP); University of Vermont.
- Malone, S. T*he Berlin Conference of 1884–1885 | Africa's Great Civilizations.* (2021, January 11). PBS LearningMedia.
- Scharmer, O. (2018, September 30). *How Are You Listening as a Leader? - Field of the Future Blog.* Medium.
- USAID. (2017, August). *Overview of the Used Clothing Market in East Africa: Analysis of Determinants and Implications.* East Africa Trade Investment Hub.
- Van Leeuwen, J., & Davis, N. (2019, January). *Community Development in Africa in an Age of Divisive Rhetoric.* Africa: Year in Review 2018. Wilson Center (Africa Program), 19.

CHAPTER TWO
Build Empathy:
Seeking to Understand Different Perspectives

LISTEN

Reinvent the Narrative

Build Empathy

Create Lasting Impact

Exchange Ideas

ACT

THINK

Innovative Through Experimentation

Forge Strong Relationships

"Community development is not about imposing your rules and ideas on another group, but listening to the real struggles and needs of a given community to develop better strategies that could be beneficial to their future progress."
- Anonymous Student, Global Scholars Fellowship Program (GLI), June 2020

Listen. Think. Act. Three words that brought us all together, through a platform we have helped build collaboratively: the Global Livingston Institute (GLI). The organization's goal of working simultaneously in the United States, Uganda, and Rwanda was not to try and "fix" a certain part of the world, but instead to help students and stakeholders from around the United States meet with their counterparts from around East Africa during lengthy immersion experiences, and to push back on that very assumption that a one-sided version of "fixing" should take place at all in community development. The intention of these immersive interactions has never been to arrive with preordained solutions in mind, but rather to bring a clear intention to simply listen and think about experiences with people we meet and about the respective communities to which we all belong. For both American and Ugandan participants, the benefit of these exchanges was to understand more about their preconceptions and to gain a more informed outlook about lifestyles elsewhere in the world. Local stakeholders engaging with students gained a platform by which to share a lived experience of East African history and culture, and to explore whether some of the students might become viable long-term collaborators in locally led community development efforts. The common thread is that people who engage across differences are regularly asked to step outside themselves and outside their comfort zones in a genuine attempt to understand someone else's perspective and experiences. In short, participants were invited to an intensive practice of empathy. This is our next lesson in community development: the importance of empathy-building and seeking to understand the perspectives of others.

———

"Street Equity," by Jamie Van Leeuwen

In the late 90s, I was a graduate student at Tulane University in New Orleans, Louisiana, working on a study for the Centers for Disease Control and Prevention (CDC) that sought to better understand the impact HIV and AIDS were having on inner cities in the United States. As a White, gay man, I knew many people who were personally affected, and I wanted to play some role in stopping the spread of this terrible epidemic. This disease was ravaging the Black and Latinx communities in New Orleans, and we were trying to better understand the impact on these communities, because those of us doing the research were not (for the most part) Black or Latinx ourselves. We were listening and thinking.

Every day I would engage in two-hour long interviews with young people addicted to heroin in a drop-in center for local youth who were experiencing homelessness. I remember sitting with this young Black man who was around my age; about 22 at the time. He was smart, funny, and charismatic, but as we conducted the interview, he would frequently drift off to sleep. He shared that he was shooting about $300 worth of heroin each day, having gotten hooked at age 11 when his uncle introduced him to the drug. The likelihood was low that this young man would live much longer, if he did not adjust his behavior.

As I later reflected on what I heard, I realized that had I, a beneficiary of various compounding privileges (White, male, cisgender), been born into this kid's family, I very well might have been the one trying to figure out where I was going to prostitute myself to get my next fix. And had this young man, who grew up amid systemic and institutionalized poverty and racism, been born into my family instead, he might have been conducting research for the CDC and pondering which trendy bar to meet his college friends at after a prolonged interview. He was smart and engaging; what he lacked were my (largely unearned) cultural and economic advantages. It is not about how intelligent you are or how hard you work; it is about structural inequity. The fact is this kid could easily have been doing what I was doing, had it not been for the overarching circumstances in which he was born and lived.

This insight came because of listening, and I shudder to think that I could have easily overlooked it. Yet this realization has informed how I have done my community development work for years since that moment.

For me, this was a "lightning bolt moment" on equity. All other variables aside, where you are born matters. The question is not just whether we level the playing field, but how will we work together to level the playing field? For me, from New Orleans in the United States to Lira in Northern Uganda, I have learned that the work should always start with seeking to understand the perspectives and experiences of different people.

———

What does the word "empathy" mean to you? How does it differ from "sympathy" or "pity," and what impact do you think it has on doing good community development work? Is it enough to just be sad when you see someone else suffering? Is it harmful to focus only on how someone else's pain made *you* feel? Once you empathize, how do you move to solidarity and action?

We need to break down the concept of empathy in real-world community development work and discuss several related topic areas, such as emotional intelligence and bias. Building on Chapter One, we will shift the perspective and provide some more specific examples from cross-cultural efforts in East Africa as we continue our community development journey.

The first use of the word "empathy" is attributed to German psychologist Theodore Lipps. In the 1880s, he coined the term "einfuhlung" (literally, "in-feeling"), to describe the emotional appreciation of another's feelings (Hardee, 2003). It involves both thinking and feeling, and sometimes even manifests as a physical reaction that our bodies have to other people when we relate to how they feel. Empathy requires that we genuinely care about and attribute value to other people and their concerns (Ditkowsky, 2020).

Having empathy can help us to recognize that we are all shaped by the environment in which we grow up and can help us see that biases and prejudices exist inside all of us to some degree. We must consistently make deliberate efforts to address our own preconceptions and avoid casting judgment as we interact with others. Whether one is a student, a tourist, a member of a local community seeking collaborative solutions to societal issues, or a community development practitioner, actively embracing new ideas and perspectives helps us gain a deeper understanding of the people and places we visit and work (Murphy, 2020).

When we do not seek to understand each other's cultures, values, and experiences, and we do not show a genuine interest in hearing all perspectives, we risk creating a reluctance on the part of stakeholders to speak genuinely about their emotions and thoughts on a given subject. More importantly, people who intervene prematurely risk exacerbating the social issues they set out to fix. This takes us back to Chapter One, and Western tendencies to act prior to understanding community needs and attaining direct community input into development work. Here are three hypothetical examples to highlight this difference in approaches:

- *Immediate Action: Would you like my old laptop?*
  - *Response: Yes! I do not have a laptop!*
- Listen and Think first...
  - Who is going to repair the laptop if it is broken?
  - What will happen to the laptop if it doesn't work?
  - How will they charge it if there is no electricity in their town?

- *Immediate Action: Would you like us to build you a new school?*
  - *Response: Yes! A school would be great!*
- Listen and Think first...
  - Are there any empty buildings that could be converted into a school?
  - Who will pay for the operations of the school once it is built?
  - Will there be enough experienced teachers to implement curriculum, and is there a sustaining funding source to pay those teachers' salaries?

- *Action: Would you like some of my clothes?*
  - *Response: Yes! Some of my best friends would like them!*
- Listen and Think first...
  - Are we creating a dependence?
  - How might we be impacting the local economy? Are we putting the local tailor out of work?
  - Do the clothes even fit? Are they in good condition? If I do not want them, why would someone else?

Empathy is a key outcome of listening and thinking very well. We listen and think so that we can understand and truly appreciate someone else's experience. If we do it right, we put ourselves into someone else's shoes to consider how our proposed action might be received and perceived. Or even how it might fail or cause harm.

———

"Humility, Mutual Respect, and Avoiding Dependencies," by: Agnes Igoye

In my experience engaging with communities and understanding perspectives of others means having mutual respect, regardless of one's level of education and socio-economic status. It requires humility and not having an imposing presence of superiority over others. It is the ability to make others feel comfortable and excited to engage in discussion. It can manifest in the way we dress and speak, or in our demeanor and body language.

My Harvard degree might help me get my foot in the door, or schedule an important meeting, but whenever I visit communities throughout my native Uganda, such credentials quickly become irrelevant if I do my job right. I listen. I ask questions. I seek to understand the problems of others. Despite my level of formal education and my privilege, the local communities remain the experts on their surroundings, their environment, and their problems.

This is what happened in 2013 when I first met with the group "Rwot Omiyo"—literally meaning "the lord has given"—in Paicho, Northern Uganda. I met with 14 women experiencing homelessness, and one man. During the LRA insurgency, the women had suffered gender-based violence and rape as a weapon of war. In that meeting, I did two things: Listen and ask questions.

"Why do you have only one man in the group?" I asked. "Because he knows how to read and write," they responded. They invited him to join their group to document their meeting decisions. Otherwise, they might have remained an all-female group.

"Why did you form Rwot Omiyo?" I asked. Their reason for creating Rwot Omiyo was to support each other through traumatic shared experiences including abduction, torture, and rape during the LRA insurgency led by rebel leader Joseph Kony. Many of them were widowed, so they took up the burden of caring for orphans/grandchildren communally, but remained homeless or with inadequate housing. For instance, one of them is a widow with six daughters who had to look for a place to sleep each night, while another widow in the group (together with her children) was sent away from her marital home by the relatives of her late husband who died after being abducted and forced to fight. She was blamed for the atrocities her husband had committed at the orders of the LRA, and others are widowed grandmothers who live in cramped huts with several grandchildren apiece.

Stigma from the community was a common concern for many of these women, who were looked at as "rebels' wives." Every member of the group had a story. They were displaced and had lost their homes and virtually all their possessions due to the conflict. They were either homeless or had inadequate access to proper housing; a basic necessity that would protect them.

After actively listening and beginning to understand their stories, I simply continued to pose questions to which they had straightforward answers. Follow-up questions and eventual solutions to their housing challenges came from the women themselves.

- Can we build those huts (houses) ourselves?
- What do we need to build them?
- Where and how can we get those materials?

By the end of the meeting, the women assigned themselves roles. They mapped out where to find the building materials, locally. This is how the *Huts for Peace* program was launched, an effort through which women build their own houses and communities. While building huts, volunteers from the community are welcomed. They share meals and experiences and talk about issues of peace and reconciliation. These communal experiences cultivate empathy, belonging, and agency.

Some members of the Rwot Omiyo group are taking care of grandchildren who lost their parents to HIV/AIDS, a significant effect of the LRA conflict. The local church donated land where they grow food to feed their children. The excess food harvested is sold in the market. This enabled them to afford health care and send the children to school.

By acting and empowering each other, the women earned invaluable respect from others in their community. This gave them the confidence to stand for office and take up leadership roles in their communities. This was a significant and sustainable change, all founded on the principles of empathy and understanding different perspectives. This experience taught me a critical lesson:

In the context of community development, respect is the ability to let other people—those most affected—drive the agenda.

Contrast this self-directed communal action with more "traditional" top-down approaches. When Northern Uganda embarked on the difficult task of reconstruction following the LRA insurgency, a lot of foreign groups and individuals arrived eager to help with donations and food supplies. Of course, these resources are critical in emergency situations. However, if sustained for long periods, this influx of free resources can create a dependency syndrome and reduce communities to becoming 'beggars.' Donations should be temporary and ultimately support the recipient communities to undertake their own programs, with local ownership and leadership. This is not to say that people should not help others in need, but there should always be thought given to unintended consequences, and to who is doing the "helping," and why.

On one of my visits to the remote region of Karamoja in northeastern Uganda, I asked the locals why there were vast acres of fertile land, yet few people were engaged in farming. The people I interacted with said that despite the nomadic nature of the Karamojong, whose livelihood is largely dependent on traditional livestock farming, the people of Karamoja have relied on food donations for so long that they are not particularly interested in engaging in new agricultural efforts.

This is why I love the example of the *Huts for Peace* program: Those women continue to build their communities day by day, supporting each other without foreign or outside assistance. In this same line of demonstrating respect and humility in development work, as a Ugandan, I applaud my nation's approach to refugee protection. Refugees in our country are given land, live in settlements side-by-side with locals, and are permitted freedom of movement. Because these refugee communities grow their own food soon after they are settled, instead of relying upon rations in perpetuity, they develop a degree of self-reliance. They are empowered.

Community development requires humility and mutual respect, especially between organizations and local communities.

———

As we introduce our next section and highlight the role that empathy plays in the practice of good community development, we highlight the journey of an American traveling to Uganda in a manner that sparked a lifelong internal dialogue about bias and our definition of what a "thriving" or "developed" community can look like.

———

"Changing My Definition of a 'Strong' Community," by: Thomas Karrel

Whenever I am diving into a conversation around community development, regardless of whether it is with a high school student or seasoned career diplomat, I always try to pose the question: "What does it really mean to have a strong community?"

I have had the privilege of being educated in the fields of international development and public health and have spent countless hours sitting in classrooms pontificating and expounding on this general question. But today, I am more critical than ever as to how we answer this question on the ground. What are we all striving for? We talk of "developed" and "developing" countries as though the former has solved all of their societal woes, and the latter are backward, passive, and helpless victims of circumstance.

As a former public health student, I am not so naive as to think that there are not some objective claims you can make regarding these questions. I believe everyone on this planet should have access to clean water, food, and shelter. No one should live in abject poverty, and there are a multitude of public health and human rights issues that need to be addressed, many of which are concentrated in the so-called "developing" world. But is that the full story when it comes to community development? Where does that narrative come from, and who gets to frame it?

I spent the first 18 years of my life in Connecticut, a state in the north-eastern United States, in a small, homogenous town where very few people I knew or encountered were struggling with the question of how to survive. The average income and lifestyle were beyond what billions of people on Earth could conceptualize. I had access to education and healthcare and never had to answer impossible questions about my safety and well-being. I could take a train ride, and in one hour I would be in the heart of New York City. My young mind believed that my hometown, and places like New York, were the pinnacle of humanity, a truly developed and enlightened society. But could there still be something missing? Were our shared goals aligned toward maximizing collective human well-being and prosperity, or toward something else entirely?

To unravel my own internal bias about development, it took me travelling to a part of the world that is all too familiar with the experience of being labeled as "behind" or "lesser than" others: East Africa, and more specifically, Uganda. My growing interest in travel and international development in college led me through several journeys to different corners of the world, but none was as impactful as the first big break of my career: a public health internship in Uganda.

For two months, alongside dozens of students from Ugandan and foreign universities, I would be working with a grassroots nonprofit organization in rural communities outside Iganga District in Eastern Uganda. In the public health world, the villages in which we were to be living and working are considered the "last mile" of health delivery: rural communities that are physically and geographically isolated from most modern health and social services.

It was here that my perception of what a strong community looks like drastically shifted. Upon arrival in Iganga, I was trained to work with a handful of colleagues from Uganda and the United States on demographic health survey data collection and community health education and partnership-building. We spent months living and breathing every aspect of a community that was as objectively different from my home in Connecticut as any inhabited place on Earth I could imagine. And in those early days, my untrained mind began to involuntarily critique the way in which people were living. This was different from the "developed" place that I grew up in.

Then I started peeling away the layers of the onion. In just the first week of living in this Ugandan village, I felt for the first time in my life that I was in the presence of a truly vibrant and connected community. Everyone knew each other, and I mean everyone. Folks were sharing household goods, livestock, and land, and conversing for hours about the beautiful simplicities of life. Time here was less bound by the number on a clock, but rather dictated by the communal activities taking place each day. Each time we visited someone's home or were invited as guests to a wedding or burial service, or attended church or a local school, we were actively welcomed by a multitude of people who clearly held values like respect and empathy at the core of their being.

This is not intended to downplay the fact that the community was lacking access to quality health and social services. But this resource deficit did not seem to stop my new neighbors from being part of a community stronger than any I had ever experienced. With every encounter I was offered mangoes, roasted groundnuts, and cups of tea, coupled with a genuine interest in who I was. This was foreign to me. If I approached a stranger in my hometown, they would most likely receive me with caution. And definitely no mangoes or groundnuts!

So, as we seek to understand the importance of empathy in community development, I go back to my question of what a strong community looks like. I used to think it looked like my financially well-off hometown in Connecticut, but now after living in different parts of Uganda for the past four years of my life and building out my empathy for these communities, I have a different take than I did before. I am sure that a strong community is one where people's well-being and happiness are paramount, and people feel connected to and respected by their neighbors and peers. The definition of "development" is often subjective and can take many forms, and it is not always tied to where a community ranks on the Human Development Index.

> *Additional Learning:* The Human Development Index (HDI) was created as a comprehensive indicator of a nation's average achievement across three key dimensions of human development: quality of life, knowledge, and standard of living. We encourage you to learn more about this indicator, along with similar tools, at the United Nations' Development Programme's website (UNDP, 2021).

I did not grow up with plans to work, let alone live, in different parts of the world. But now that I have done so, I can see that there are so many intangible aspects to building strong communities, and I am more curious than ever to investigate further what those are for different people. And I believe empathy is at the core of this journey of discovery.

———

When you travel outside your own immediate circle, whether that be to a different neighborhood, a different town, or an entirely different continent, your familiarity or unfamiliarity with the community you seek to interact with plays an important part in how you do your work. One's "cultural competence" can be distilled down to an ability to understand one's own culture and the implications it may have when interacting with people across a difference in cultures. This is done by demonstrating an ethical and effective understanding of the other party's perspective in relation to one's own to foster a respectful and reflective relationship or collaboration (Sherwood, 2017). This concept is not exclusive to someone getting on an airplane for 24 hours and travelling across the globe to a new country or continent. In the United States or Uganda, it can merely take a car ride or even a bicycle trip to encounter a community with different values, beliefs, or ways of living, and to highlight the need for cultural competence.

A concrete example of where this commonly goes awry today is in the misconceptions held in the United States and Europe regarding the continent of Africa that we referenced in Chapter One. When working in the United States, we encounter people all the time who view Africa as a homogenous region characterized by strife and misery. It is vital to reframe this one-dimensional view. The author Chimamanda Ngozi Adichie, who lives in both Nigeria and America, frames this idea well in her viral TED Talk, "The Danger of a Single Story" (Adichie, 2009). She explains that if someone only learns about a person, place, or event from one point of view, they are at risk of accepting this narrative as the entire truth: a "single story". This narrow perspective can be very dangerous, as it is often expressed based on assumptions and incomplete impressions, and breeds bias and prejudice towards other cultures and communities.

How are we so easily swayed to jump from one stereotype to the all-encompassing single story that Adichie references? And could these stories we tell ourselves about other communities affect the way we do development work? Absolutely. Gaining extensive insight into the perspectives and beliefs of a given population is paramount in community development work. And the best way to do this is through building empathy and asking questions of people from different backgrounds and socioeconomic statuses. Don't just do something ... stand there.

Our biases can be incredibly dangerous, create social barriers, and have the power to negatively impact entire cultures, communities, groups of people, and regions of the world. So, how do we begin to overcome them? In her lecture, "How to overcome our biases? Walk boldly toward them," American activist Verna Myers argues that we first need to acknowledge the existence and extent of our biases, and then begin to move toward, not away from, the groups or interactions that make us uncomfortable (Myers, 2014). This point applies to all our experiences working in community development. Building empathy and challenging our assumptions is not easy! Quite the opposite. It takes genuine commitment, training, self-awareness, and humility to lean in and "face the music." In doing so we must admit when we have internalized misinformation and when we do not know the right answers. The first step is a careful examination of our own assumptions. But before chastising ourselves or others for having prejudices (as we all bring them to our community development work), it is critical that we first talk about them. We need to understand where the false narratives come from, and through empathetic interactions begin engaging more deeply with people who come from different communities and perspectives. Whenever we find ourselves at a table, or invited into a decision-making process, empathy compels us to look around the room and ask ourselves, "who is not here who should be? And why were they not invited to begin with?"

————

"Seeking to Understand the Perspectives of Others is to Recognize Diversity," by: Agnes Igoye

I often remind some of my non-African friends that Africa is not a country; it's a beautifully diverse continent of 54 nations. Even within one country, a demonym (e.g. "Ugandan") is often an over-generalization: my home nation of Uganda is about the size of the state of Oregon, yet it contains 56 different tribes, all speaking different languages, with unique cultural practices and behaviors. I can only speak three of those languages. Does that make me an expert in all communities throughout Uganda? I'll let you figure out the answer to that one. Along the same lines, I constantly remind my fellow Ugandans that the United States is incredibly diverse, culturally, and geographically. Imagining the United States as one uniform cultural and demographic entity is doing the same disservice as grouping Uganda, let alone all of Africa, in similarly homogenous terms.

Diversity is part of human nature. This is a reminder of the importance of listening to diverse voices and the perspectives of all people, regardless of age, gender, and cultural affiliation. When you are looking at a specific issue or geographic area, every perspective needs to be heard if we are going to succeed in crafting sound solutions to complicated developmental challenges.

This is what I had in mind when I reached out to the Member of Parliament (MP) in my hometown of Pallisa, in Eastern Uganda. I come from a highly patriarchal community, and it's the men who generally speak at meetings. They are the ones who mainly determine how their communities are run and what development projects to prioritize. Building empathy and seeking to understand the perspectives of others requires that we learn about community power dynamics; this also requires consideration of whose voices are typically not solicited. It also requires us to recognize our positions of privilege. In my own community, it helps if I recognize my position of privilege as an educated woman and listen more intently when I interact with others in the community.

One day, I challenged my MP to call a special village meeting and give women the opportunity to speak. Let them set the agenda and establish priorities for their community. Men were required to simply listen as the women spoke. To his credit, the MP accepted my challenge and called the meeting as I suggested.

When we arrived for the meeting, we initially found men seated on the benches, waiting. I asked the MP whether he had sent the wrong message regarding who we were targeting to attend the meeting. Then I asked the gentlemen where the women were, to which they replied: "They are still collecting water; some are in the garden and others are collecting firewood. They first want to make sure they complete their household duties before attending the meeting."

From a distance we could see women walking in a hurry with pots of water on their heads, weaving their hoes through gardens, and carrying bundles of firewood, clearly making haste upon hearing that their MP had arrived, and they were needed at the meeting. From this observation, even before commencement of the meeting, one could see that women as cultivators are needed as experts on food security. They are well positioned to talk about climate change, and the effects of changing weather patterns on their harvests. They are well positioned to talk about energy-efficient technologies, since they are the ones often searching for firewood or charcoal for cooking. They are well positioned to talk about the health of their children, since they are the ones who take care of little ones. They are well positioned to discuss water safety, because they are the ones often carrying water pots from wells that lie far away from their homes. And yes, these women are well positioned to talk about family planning, because they are the ones who access the services and experience the side effects.

Eventually, the women arrived, and the meeting began. It took the men a while to stop interrupting the women as they spoke. When they eventually felt they were being listened to, the women voiced their perspectives and shared their own realities. This was not just on behalf of these women alone; they spoke for interventions that they felt would benefit the whole community. They spoke of health care, improving household incomes, education, and support to people with disabilities. They were able to communicate about family planning methods that caused devastating effects to women in the community. The male MP looked stunned, because the men in his constituency who often spoke at meetings had never raised any of these issues. Family planning services were not a priority for the men because it was mainly the women who utilized the services, I reminded him.

This moment highlighted a collective effort not to judge, but simply to put oneself in other people's shoes. By giving women a voice in the patriarchal community of Pallisa, our MP tried to put himself in their shoes. To build genuine empathy.

Another group whose views are often ignored is that of children—especially in the world of politics—because they cannot formally vote. Children who are growing up in what Americans and Europeans call the "developing" world are especially sidelined and treated as props or objects for pity. It is far too common to see pictures of poor children in the foreign news media, rather than hearing their opinions, views, and testimonials about the subject matter being covered. Their photos are often taken without consent. The more torn their clothing and sadder their facial expressions, the better it is for raising money to support entities that are located overseas and say they do "development." This is a reality I have encountered far too many times.

Compiling ideas and opinions directly from children is what drove me to launch the *End Child Trafficking* campaign. According to Uganda's 2009 Prevention of Trafficking in Persons Act, child trafficking constitutes sexual exploitation of children, child marriage, harmful child labor, use of children in armed conflict, child sacrifice, removal of organs or body parts for sale, witchcraft, and rituals (UC Berkeley School of Law, 2009). To support children's participation in creating awareness about a challenge that affects them, I involved a group of community artists. The children wanted to tell child trafficking stories, through art and community theater. The only instruction we gave to the children was to define what exactly constitutes child trafficking. The community artists supported these kids as they designed costumes and built their confidence to appear on stage. Something amazing took place: based on what they had witnessed in their own communities, the children produced scripts, stories, poems and plays, depicting child exploitation that was prevalent in their communities. They showcased their own talents while also creating awareness about the effects of child trafficking in their communities.

Children are highly effective communicators when empowered to tell their own stories. The children from Northern Uganda chose the topic of 'the use of children in armed conflict' and made toy guns out of banana fibers and sticks and acted out scenes that involved child abduction. The children from Eastern Uganda chose 'child marriage' as their topic. They recited poems and acted out their plays at marketplaces and at schools to raise awareness among their peers and teachers.

We captured these messages, recorded videos, and showed them to Uganda's top policy makers. Now this was impactful. The children were able to have their voices heard. Some of them were invited to stage their performances to mark International Women's Day for thousands to see. These were powerful messages and portrayals of systemic community development issues that these children wanted to address.

Our intention was to give these children a space and opportunity to express themselves that they had never been given. We were simply seeking to understand their perspectives, but something else transpired as well: the children found their voices and were encouraged to use them. Just like the women being invited to the table by the MP, these children were engaged as equal participants worthy of consideration, dignity, and respect. This is not just academic, or a "nice to have." Our work suffers when we exclude necessary perspectives from the conversation. Without these voices, we waste money, we waste time, and we squander opportunity.

———

Our societies tend to draw imaginary lines in the sand between ourselves and other groups of people. As we saw in the previous story, this can cause a lot of damage or limit the perceived potential of a certain community.

We see this all the time in our work, with various organizations and people referring to communities different from their own as "them", taking us back to Adichie's danger of a single story. This is not limited to international work. There are many connections to be made here about having difficult conversations in community development work in our home countries as well as in other parts of the world.

There is a wonderful story that highlights an extreme case of this in the United States. Michael Kent, a former self-identified White supremacist from Arizona, completely reformed his life after sparking an unexpected friendship with Tiffany Whittier, his Black parole officer (Revesz, 2017). Kent had spent 20 years of his life as a member of a violent White supremacist group, and it wasn't until being paired with a parole officer of another race that he realized he had been completely wrong in his perceptions. In fact, he had never actually spent any significant time getting to know a person of a different race. It took a Black woman genuinely interested in his well-being to make a positive impact on Kent's life. Being exposed (even involuntarily) to someone who did not judge him and who had his best interests at heart allowed Kent to let go of his old ideas and completely transform his life and belief system. Kent had discriminatory tattoos removed from his body and shared that he now "views Whittier as family."

Additional Learning: "Only the soul that ventilates the world with tenderness has any chance of saving the world." In his 2018 keynote address to the students at Pepperdine University, Father Gregory Boyle, Founder of Homeboy Industries, provides a powerful example of how the "Us" and "Them" Paradigm can create harmful distance and misguided judgment between communities. Boyle tells the story of a young man named Mario, a former gang member who is covered in gang-related tattoos; Mario goes through the unique experience of walking around streets and seeing people passing by with nervous looks upon seeing him, clutching their children, and avoiding his path. Father Boyle points out a staggering juxtaposition, claiming that Mario "is the kindest, most gentle soul who works at Homeboy Industries." You can find this specific clip of Boyle's speech on YouTube titled "One of The Most Inspirational Speeches From Gangsters," which highlights the damaging distance that biases and lack of empathy can place between people (Boyle, 2019).

Seemingly insurmountable cultural gaps can sometimes be overcome through simple and genuine interactions between people from different communities. It all starts with a legitimate attempt to build empathy for each other, beginning with a willingness to listen.

On your journey into community development work, before jumping to conclusions about another neighborhood or another region, try to turn the mirror inward. Would you consider most of your friends, community members, or co-workers to be culturally competent? If so, why do you think that is? If not, how could you go about changing that? How would you build empathy?

Do Your Homework

Preparation is key in seeking to understand the perspectives of other communities. Prior to visiting a region or implementing new community development projects, endeavor to understand the culture and the history of the people you hope to engage. Read books, preferably those written by people from countries and communities you intend to engage in. Become familiar with the languages, the music, and the arts of the region. Learn the rituals; build an appreciation for how the community celebrates and how it grieves. Building empathy helps to establish effective collaborations but can also be personally enlightening. Even if you have read the books and seen the movies and listened to the music, your job is never done. Empathy requires a near-constant humility, a willingness to admit that there is always more to learn, and always another perspective to consider. If you ever find yourself thinking you know all there is to know about a topic or a community, seek out perspectives that might differ from your own. Challenge yourself to see your subject from a different angle. Poke holes in your own expertise.

———

"Misguided History Lessons from Abroad," by: Agnes Igoye

I was once in the company of an American; he was a White man who was visiting Uganda for the first time. One of our conversations turned into an argument regarding things that had occurred in Uganda's history. Now, it is important to understand that I was alive and present for the events in question. I told him about events that had happened when I was a teenager. He discounted my views, claiming that he had read another interpretation of events from an authority he trusted. A book written by an American about Uganda.

Could he not see how that might make me feel upset? This inhibited a potential friendship and productive dialogue between the two of us. I wished that he would have allowed my side of the story to be fully heard, before establishing an unshakable conclusion. Although my story contradicted his own initial understanding, he should not have instantly shut me out. For the record, I have nothing against books written by foreigners about Uganda, but understanding perspectives other than our own requires that we actually listen and acknowledge the perspectives of other people. We all experience things differently.

We also all need to be conscious of the lasting effects of colonialism and racism in international community development work. I once interacted with a Peace Corps volunteer who was posted to a village in rural Uganda to teach. The volunteer, an African American woman, was going to a community where a White Peace Corps volunteer had previously served. She was particularly excited to connect with the community and to reconnect with part of her heritage as a Black woman. But when she arrived, she was saddened to find that some members of the community were disappointed; they were expecting a White American. They preferred White to Black. Based on past examples, the local community had a strong perception that White people would bring money, resources, and help for them. When this new woman came in, her Black skin was unfairly judged as associating her with an alternative narrative; someone with fewer resources and less potential to help.

Effects of colonialism are still, unfortunately, alive, and well. I have had many meals with White American friends in restaurants in my own country where waiters chose to serve my White friends before me, even when I was the first to arrive at the restaurant. Recognizing their privilege, my American friends are often quick to point it out, and tell the waiter to serve me first, to—empathetically, in their view—right a wrong on my behalf. Is this the best way to handle such a situation? Does someone else speaking up empower me? Or does the way in which a White person tries to take charge in such circumstances actually disempower both me and the waiter? And if my White friend is a man, does this reassert the patriarchal system that I address in my own work? How can we tackle these problems together? Perhaps friends could consult with me before acting? There are so many questions to be answered when thinking about empathy and the role it plays in community development.

In another instance, I was checking into a hotel in Entebbe, Uganda, for a week-long workshop as a consultant to train law enforcement officials. The gentleman at check-in was extremely professional until a White couple arrived, one of them waving their hotel key, claiming it had stopped working. They disregarded the fact that I was being served, and the gentleman at the counter decided to abandon me to attend to the White couple. When they left, I used the moment as an educational opportunity, which the gentleman took in good faith. He was able to realize and acknowledge that he wouldn't have done it if the couple was Black. But here, I was able to achieve an actual dialogue with the other party; a moment in which we both got to voice our thoughts.

I have often had tough and honest conversations with my fellow Ugandans about this. Each of us has had our "aha!" liberation moments, letting go of misconceptions as to our inferiority in our own society due to the color of our skin. Regardless of our race, each of us must constantly recognize and strive to overcome internalized biases and stereotypes.

Before I arrived in the United States for the first time, the opinions I had about the country were mainly derived from what I saw on television and read in books. I was anticipating beautiful buildings, snow, hurricanes, and Hollywood. I remember being surprised that people rarely kissed in public like I had seen in so many movies. I was shocked to see homeless people in Los Angeles, California, the entertainment capital of the world. Over a lengthy period, during which I had the chance to study at the University of Minnesota and at Harvard University, I found my ideas evolving. The more I interacted with Americans, the more I got to know about the diversity of the country, which far exceeded the single story that my television had told me.

Like the young man I encountered who thought he knew more than I did about the community where I grew up and the history of the region that I call home, my early impressions of America were defined by my own cultural lens. It was through empathy-building and open conversations that I was able to correct some of the misperceptions I carried about the community of which I was now a part.

These experiences have ultimately had a positive ending for me. They have challenged me to not only speak, but also write and document my own stories; stories about my lived experiences, my community; first-hand perspectives working as a migration and development practitioner. These experiences drove me to learn the craft and ultimately become a better writer and communicator. I have since gone on to write nationally and internationally so others can appreciate perspectives from people who look like me and have endured similar experiences.

———

There is an old joke that goes like this:

> What do you call someone who speaks two languages? *Bilingual.*
> What do you call someone who speaks three languages? *Trilingual.*
> What do you call someone who only speaks one language? *American.*

No one language or form of communication is superior to others. This can take a lot of humility to understand—especially for native English speakers—but is a vital part in our quest to build empathy and a critical ingredient to good community development.

The art of listening is a skill, and to perfect a skill requires practice. Listening takes a lot of practice and is easier said than done in the context of community development. Many Americans, Europeans, and some Africans who live in former British colonies have chosen to make English the dominant language used in efforts at cross-cultural exchange. But if English is not your first language, it can be especially hard to pick up on nuanced humor or inflection.

Words matter, and so do the means of communication. Sometimes the meaning of particular words gets lost in translation. Words may also carry alternative meanings when they are applied in a different location. Actively listening to understand slang and idioms helps to prevent possible misinterpretations. If English is not the first language of a given community, try to learn some of the commonly spoken languages used by those with whom you want to collaborate. If you cannot take the time to become fluent, learn even a few words, such as please and thank you.

Active listening also goes beyond the spoken word and is augmented by body language. Skilled listeners pick up emotional cues from facial expressions, tone of voice, and other non-verbal communications that better inform us about the work that we are doing (SkillsYouNeed, 2021). In the absence of active listening and an informed awareness of subtle cultural cues, one can convey insincerity or pretense, even when that might not be intended.

Remember, non-verbal expression can vary immensely across cultures, so simply paying attention may not always be sufficient as it is easy to misinterpret what we are observing. For example, an American spending time interacting with Ugandans might be confused when they ask a question, and instead of a verbal response, their friend simply raises their eyebrows. This is a common gesture in Uganda. An eyebrow raise can mean affirmation, although to that American it may seem like the Ugandan is trying to suggest arousal or simply ignoring their question altogether!

Additional Learning: Explore the concept of Emotional Intelligence. How able are you to identify your emotions and those of the people around you? Would you say you manage emotions well? A high level of emotional intelligence means you can read other people's emotions skillfully, and you are in tune with what you are feeling and how your emotions affect other people. Being aware of one's own emotional intelligence is particularly important when travelling and interacting with people from different countries and backgrounds. For further learning on this topic, we recommend checking out Ramona Hacker's lecture, "Six steps to improve your emotional intelligence." You will hear her personal journey towards realizing the importance of emotional intelligence, and how it affects our communities and the way we deal with our problems.

Empathy Cannot Be Faked

Understanding people's feelings and concerns requires time. It is not about dropping into a community for a few minutes, seizing the moment with a photo opportunity, ticking the "community consultation box," and then leaving in a hurry. Professional ethnographers—those who study and research human cultures—spend months, usually years, studying a single community, and may understand this better than anyone. Even with years of expertise in anthropology and human-centered studies, top research professionals still face challenges in how to develop truly authentic relationships with the communities they observe and work with (Cavanagh, 2005).

Students and development workers who are adept at building empathy and who spend substantial periods of time in communities foster a more in-depth cultural understanding of how to do development work. They explore what it is like to actually be a member of a community. They ask nuanced and difficult questions. They attend weddings and funerals and baptisms. They pay attention to the mundane—a visit to the produce market or a trip using public transportation—as well as to the big picture. They live in the same way as local community members, and through these immersive experiences they begin to understand concerns at the most basic and fundamental level. They listen and think and interact with people over time. They take on the hard task of building empathy with the people and communities where they work.

———

"Not All Survivors of Human Trafficking Want to Make Paper Beads,"
by: Agnes Igoye

I once said this to a large international gathering of professionals who specialize in protection and rehabilitation work for victims of human trafficking. At that point, many organizations involved in rehabilitation work in Uganda were pushing survivors to make beads for female clients in the Western market, especially the US, as an economically viable model for income generation. Now, I have nothing against asking survivors to make beads as a means of therapy or generating income, but we must be aware of something: all survivors are unique individuals, with different interests and skill sets. One survivor I spoke with was stressed because she was required to make beads that met the required high standards of the Western market. They worked long, hard hours, and the brutal irony was that making beads became another form of exploitation, with pressure on survivors to satisfy an external market. Survivors, just like any other beneficiaries of development assistance, must always be consulted to ensure they participate in activities of their choice.

In my work, I have trained thousands of law enforcement personnel about how to identify victims of human trafficking and how to investigate those crimes. I also travel around the world to create awareness about these issues. One of the most important things that I have learned is that you cannot stop trafficking if you do not take good care of survivors. You cannot expect a survivor to go to court and help law enforcement officers in their efforts to seek justice if the survivor is sick, or hungry, or does not have adequate shelter. And food, shelter, and health care all require money.

One of the main reasons people wind up as victims of trafficking in the first place is that they do not have good jobs. Traffickers target low-skilled workers. They lure them with false promises of better employment, and then the victims wind up being forced into prostitution or becoming domestic workers in foreign countries. What women need most of all, to be able to resist human trafficking in the first place, is access to good jobs. And what they need most if they are survivors is also access to good jobs. You can learn this by speaking directly with these women and seeking to understand their situation at a deeper level.

———

Here we turn to a sensitive topic in community development and something that each of us writing this book has struggled with at times. There is a fine line between building empathy and practicing voyeurism. In this context, we look at "voyeurism" as exploiting people less fortunate for one's own gain or glorifying the strife and hardships that others face. Wrestling with this concept is not a challenge limited to those in formal development circles, but something that all members of society should face, particularly when traveling to different communities and countries.

Each of us still ponders our own actions in light of this concept when we go into the Katanga community, commonly referred to as a "slum," in downtown Kampala, or when we visit with former child soldiers in Lira. To do this work, you must understand the populations you work with. To teach students about good community development, you can ask them to read extensively, but then eventually the students must experience the work. You have to touch it and taste it and feel it. There is a needle to thread regarding how you learn about good community development and start to build empathy, without falling into the trap that is voyeurism. And as we will explore further in Chapter Four, one of the determining factors is the quality of the relationships that you build. Are all parties served well by the interaction? Is there open dialogue about whether this is the case? Are the parties able to be honest with each other, or is there a power differential in play that stifles conversation?

Going to a slum for a day to look at poor people and to glimpse the conditions they are living in is voyeurism. Actively engaging in the community for years at a time, forging lasting relationships with those who live there, and constantly working to make sure the relationships serve all parties as well as humanly possible in a deeply flawed world is an exercise in empathy-building. Going to Lira to see where former child soldiers live and to talk to them for a few hours about their experiences of being an abductee is voyeurism. Working with former child soldiers over an extended period to help them heal from trauma is an exercise in empathy building. If it feels as though you are treating the communities you speak of serving like a human zoo—where the experience is one in which you look through the window of tragedy onto people's daily lives, yet never get past the glass of the window yourself—then you need to revisit your approach. These interactions may be truly damaging for those persons under the gaze, whose perspectives on the interaction are rarely heard by the visitors. This is not good community development, and this is not building empathy.

We have had to figure this out ourselves. Sometimes we get it right, and other times we do not. To learn how to work with street-based populations and people experiencing homelessness, eventually as part of your training you should see how a detox operates, you should know a lot about the day-to-day operations of a homeless shelter, and you should understand the process of how a person moves in and out of the local jail. Along the way, you should develop the capacity to imagine yourself in the position of a homeless person with some correlation between your ideas and reality. We would worry about hiring someone straight out of a master's program who wanted to work with the homeless, but who had never visited a shelter. There is an obvious disconnect between the theoretical belief in service and a real understanding of the lived experience of those who will be on the receiving end of that intended impact.

To learn, you must experience. But to gain the right kind of experience, and to learn as much as possible from it, you must once again listen and think before you act. We learned from our own mistakes that engaging in the Katanga slum community in Kampala needed to be about the relationships we formed and how well we connected to others. Before you can show up and research and study and understand the dynamics of the slum, you need to connect with leaders of the community and understand how they operate. You need to build relationships and establish a mutual understanding about what the community's goals are and what work the grassroots members of the community are doing. There needs to be an exchange of information and a true learning experience, as opposed to the dreaded act of "philanthro-tourism" complete with photo opportunities and cheap gifted footballs. Over the years, we have built relationships with leaders and community members in the Katanga community, and they in turn have taught us a lot about the needs of the people who live there. Together, we have worked on ways to give back through improved access to public health services and community-building efforts.

The same goes for our collaborations with the former child soldiers in Lira. Over time, we came to know the community and the former abductees through hosting a series of music festivals at which we offered public health interventions in addition to music and dance. They let us into their world, and we listened with them and thought with them about how we could work together more collaboratively and learn from each other.

This is not to say that there cannot ever be an exchange of soccer balls and selfies. But that exchange must be mutual and shared and it must unfold over time. Community development is not about showing up for a few hours and taking pictures of babies alongside open sewage to show the world how bad things are. We would not want someone to show up at our house or our neighborhood park and take pictures of our children to broadcast to other people without our permission. We would not want others to pity us based on depictions gathered on days when we are not at our best. Those of us in community development owe community members the same courtesy.

————

"Empathy and Truth Come from the People You Serve," by: Jamie Van Leeuwen

Having begun the journey of becoming an expert in homelessness, and having opened the door just a crack, I was orchestrating our third Project Homeless Connect in Denver, where we connected the business community with the unhoused and we connected the unhoused with services, all in one day.

At one point during Project Homeless Connect, we were on our way to pick up a group of guests at the Gathering Place, a women's day shelter in Denver, to take them to the Convention Center where they would participate in the event. A reporter joined us to see how this all worked. A woman got on the bus with her beautiful two-year old kid. As we made our way back to the event, I asked her what three things she hoped to get out of the day's event for herself and her son.

But in my mind, I already knew what those three things were. I was an expert on homelessness, and I had been doing this work for a decade. Homeless mom and kid. Let us not just stand there … but do something! She needs a job, she needs housing, and we need to get her, and her son, signed up for benefits. And that should get the job done. That should solve a big chunk of her problems.

She looked at me and told me that she needed all those things, but then paused. She said that while she knew those things were important, that is not what kept her up at night. She went on to tell me that since her son was born, they had stayed in abandoned buildings and the back seats of cars; they had slept in elevator shafts and on friends' couches and in family shelters. And in the two years since her kid was born, they had never stayed at the same place for more than a week.

What kept this mother up at night was the social well-being of her son. She was worried that he would grow up without ever having any friends of his own, as they never stayed in the same place for more than a week. And she asked me, if possible, when we found that unit of housing for her, if we could make sure it was within walking distance of a playground. They had never lived within walking distance of a playground.

Well… shit. We missed that one. Our 'Ten Year Plan to End Homelessness' was filled with numbers and innovations and well-thought-out strategies for how to end homelessness. But there was nothing in there about playgrounds. What this mom wanted for her kid was what every parent wants for their kids, and what my parents made sure they provided for me: a slide, a swing set, and a central gathering place for kids his age. She wanted more than services and housing. She wanted to improve her son's quality of life, not just by accessing a job or health care benefits, but through human interaction and genuine empathy.

———

Building empathy is about getting to know the people you are working with. Seeking to understand communities other than your own takes time. You cannot just show up, get what you need, and leave. Community development is not a one-day visit, and it should be done with respect and humility. Take a selfie with someone using the same level of respect you would bring to taking a picture with your best friend. Engage in a pick-up game of soccer or spend an afternoon at someone's home, but extend the same level of dignity you would extend to your neighbors at their home. Practicing community development with empathy is not so much about who you engage, but how you engage.

Summing Up

There are not many college courses that teach about building empathy. Yet empathy is a core part of good community development (and, truly, good work of any kind). How successful you are in building empathy depends on how well you listen and how culturally competent you become about the communities where you seek to work. Without empathy, we are bound to make unnecessary mistakes and to misinterpret the issues facing the communities we want to engage in. Failure to master this skill, or to take the time necessary to practice it, will result in missed opportunities or even worse, real harm. You do not have to spend ten years living in a community to build empathy that can inform your work, although doing so would certainly deepen your understanding (but not make you infallible). When working across cultures there may be facets that require a decade or more to comprehend. But regardless of how long you have been in a community or how long you plan to stay, you must listen and develop a keen sense of cultural sensitivities, language, and norms before you stop standing there and start doing something. Empathy is a tool you need to have in your toolbox if you want to do good community development. Without it, nothing else works.

Our next section will move us beyond listening, and into thinking.

CHAPTER TWO "COMMUNITY CHANGEMAKER" CHALLENGE: EMPATHIZE

Now that you have identified your community, area of interest and user(s), it's time to dive deeper into the empathize phase of Chapter Two.

- Start by doing secondary research, compiling existing information. Explore the literature, via the internet or local library for more background on your community and area of interest and gain a more comprehensive understanding of the issue. Understand the issue on individual, interpersonal, and institutional levels.
- Brainstorm questions to ask people in the target community. After you do this, review the questions for bias/preconceptions and adjust accordingly. It is always a good idea to have other colleagues review your questions and give the subsequent responses from community members the same review for biases/preconceptions.
- Now, push beyond your comfort zone, hit the streets, and jump into some primary research. Begin by having conversations with real users in your community. This can be informal at first. The aim is to learn about the user in detail. Ask questions! Listen.
  - If you find a person who seems comfortable speaking with you, ask politely if they would like to participate in an interview. You will want to explain why you are seeking to understand their circumstances.
    - Is there a beneficial outcome your counterpart can expect from your relationship?
    - What might that be?
    - Can you share that possibility?
  - If they seem comfortable with being asked some preliminary questions, then you may want to ask follow-up questions. Keep in mind, sometimes your questions reflect what you yourself assume to be important, which is not necessarily what your respondents think is

important. If you plan to use their responses in your work, you will have to take notes! Here are some tips to help guide your interviews:
- Ask why?
- Encourage story sharing.
- Do not be afraid of silence.
- Pay attention to non-verbal cues.
- Never say "usually" when asking questions (this can introduce unnecessary biases and influence responses).
- Look for inconsistencies (these can provide clues to understanding the nuances and complexities of the community).
- Do not suggest answers to your questions.
- Utilize all your senses to truly empathize with your user. We recommend the 'empathy map' tool, which can be accessed free from IDEO on their website) (Kelly, 2018).
- Be open to the conversation moving in unexpected directions.
  - After you finish your work, try thinking out loud with a mentor or colleague about how your research went:
    - How do you think you made participants feel while you were conducting interviews?
    - What might it have been like to receive your questions?
    - What is "active listening," and did you do this in your work?
    - What does it sound like to verbalize empathy, and were you able to do so during your exchange?
    - How might you become even more culturally competent in the future?
    - What did you learn that was surprising to you?

Your objective in this section is to challenge your biases, let go of preconceived notions, and listen intently to your end users from the community. Do not think too far into what you learn at this stage. For now, just capture everything that you can. Remember to ask yourself how you can evolve. Ultimately, one of the most interesting things you can learn from someone, is what they think is important for their community!

CHAPTER TWO CONVERSATION STARTERS

- What is your own definition of empathy?
- How did Thomas's story of redefining a strong community resonate with you?
- Think about a time when you have been able to build empathy for

someone else. What did that feel like? Describe the process and compare your experience with others.

- How do Agnes' stories from her community development work in Uganda and Jamie's stories from his community development work in the United States resonate with you?
- How might you translate the lessons from Chapter Two into your own community development work?
- If you could share with everyone in the world one lesson, as it relates to empathy and biases, what would it be? Why?
- How do you think the historical context of your home community affects today's problems?
- Do you think issues surrounding historical context are being properly addressed in development work happening in your community?

CHAPTER TWO ADDITIONAL RECOMMENDED CONTENT

- Boyle, G. (2019, January 25). *One of The Most Inspirational Speeches From Gangsters | Father Gregory Boyle.* Pepperdine University Keynote Address. YouTube.
- Collier, P. (2008). *The Bottom Billion: Why the Poorest Countries are Failing and What Can Be Done About It* (1st ed.). Oxford University Press.
- Dallaire, R. (2003, September). *Shake Hands with The Devil: The Failure of Humanity in Rwanda.* Random House Canada.
- Dolan, E. W. (2015, April 16). *New study confirms Mark Twain's saying: Travel is fatal to prejudice.* PsyPost.
- Goleman, D. (1995). *Emotional Intelligence: Why It Can Matter More Than IQ (Leading with Emotional Intelligence)* (Abridged ed.). Bantam Books.
- Gourevitch, P. (1999). *We Wish to Inform You That Tomorrow We Will be Killed with Our Families: Stories from Rwanda* (First ed.). Picador.
- Hochschild, A. (1999). *King Leopold's Ghost: A Story of Greed, Terror, and Heroism in Colonial Africa.* Mariner Books.
- Igoye, A., Karrel, T., Van Leeuwen, J. (2020, January). *Africa's Migration: Embracing Free Movement of Persons Amidst a Changing Migration and Refugee Climate in the United States.* Africa: Year in Review 2019. Wilson Center (Africa Program), 21.
- Rice, A. (2010). *The Teeth May Smile but the Heart Does Not Forget: Murder and Memory in Uganda* (First ed.). Picador.
- Sirolli, E. (2012, November 26). *Want to help someone? Shut up and listen!* TED Talks.

- Van Leeuwen, J., Miller, L., Amanya, J., & Feinberg, M. (2018, March). *Forced to Fight: An Integrated Approach to Former Child Soldiers in Northern Uganda.* Wilson Center (Africa Program).
- Van Leeuwen, J., Miller, L., Zamir, M., Grundy, R., Amanya, J., Chen, C., & Feinberg, M. (2018). *Community reintegrating former child soldiers in Northern Uganda: A qualitative study on the road to recovery.* Journal of Psychology in Africa, 28(2), 105–109. https://doi.org/10.10 80/14330237.2018.1454580.

PART II: THINK

In Part II, THINK, we delve deeper into the community development process, and discuss the components that are paramount to building a solid foundation for long-term success: strong relationships that enable genuine idea exchange or thinking in concert. This section explores the stages when organizations and individuals take time to download extensive research and insights, discuss them with their peers and colleagues, and ultimately, work smarter. Wherever you are in the world, thinking with, not for, community members and target audiences is what separates the good community development work from the bad.

Community transformation is born the very moment behavioral change begins to take effect. To influence people to think and make decisions immobilizes their communal challenges. Don't think for people, think with them."
- Humphrey Nabimanya, Founder and Team Leader, Reach a Hand Uganda

CHAPTER THREE
Exchange Ideas:
Having Important Conversations
About Societal Issues

"*The 'if we can put a man on the moon' boosterism glosses over the reality that building rockets and building livable communities are two fundamentally different endeavors: the former requires uncanny narrow focus; the latter must engage a holistic view. Building a livable world isn't rocket science; it's far more complex than that.*"
- Ed Ayres, God's Last Offer (2001)

We found the passage above from Canadian author and social activist Naomi Klein's book, This Changes Everything, and ever since it has been stuck in our heads (Klein, 2015). In Klein's case, she is referring directly to our world's battle with the climate crisis, but the point rings equally true in all forms of community development. Community development is not rocket science, because it cannot be boiled down to specific equations or be easily transferred in numeric form across cultural and geographical boundaries. In many ways, community development is far more complex than rocket science, because the listening, thinking, and acting involved belong to an entirely different type of human endeavor, and they will look different each time you do it. Please do not tell any rocket scientists that we said that!

In Part I, we stressed the importance of listening and seeking to understand before trying to teach others. We have now spent time sharing stories, looking to understand, and building empathy with target communities. By this point, you should have a better sense that the listening processes of good community development take a lot of work and a lot of time. As we said in Chapter Two, it is an imprecise science and the complexities involved can not only lead you astray but can also evoke new emotions as you are working with vulnerable communities and people. With good community development work comes a lot of responsibility.

Part II is about the art of thinking and stresses the importance of exchanging ideas through critical conversations. The context you are working in matters and creating spaces for balanced and open conversations about real-world problems and their contextual causes can be challenging. Expanding on the importance of sharing stories in Chapter One and building empathy in Chapter Two, Chapter Three takes a closer look at the conversations that help turn stories and problems into innovative ideas and positive change. As these ideas come to fruition and as we look for resources to implement them, we also turn our attention to the critical aspects of foreign aid and the concept of neo-colonialism as it relates to the continent of Africa.

The Arduous Process of Thinking

There is so much to be learned, no matter how small or localized the target community is. That is why community development is not an exact science. You cannot create specific responses to real-world issues without experiencing them yourself in some way. When you do this work, there will be moments or even days where you experience fatigue from the work that you take on. You need to think about it, talk about it, and really mull it over. After all of that listening, you are now at the juncture of your community development work where you need to think critically about what you are learning and the work that you propose to do. How you go about this process will determine the success of your action phase. No pressure, but thinking is very important!

Your objectives in this phase of your community development should be to ignite thoughtful and vital conversations around issues facing the communities where you are working. You might assume that idea exchange and thought-provoking conversations are embedded in all community development work, but that simply is not the case. Community development too often takes place in a vacuum where action is guided by good intentions and uninformed assumptions without sufficient input from the community. In essence, it is sloppy community development. Why does this happen under the guise of organizations that were designed at their core to improve the health and well-being of the people they serve?

First, community development practitioners are not typically incentivized to prioritize this stage. In their defense, there are not always a lot of resources allocated to support this front-end work, even though we would argue it is the most important determinant of success. Donors and investors want impact. They want numbers and outcomes, and they often structure their requests with short timeframes that limit the ability to fully engage in both listening and thinking. Some argue that time is of the essence and much of the community development work that is done can have significant human consequences. We do not disagree. The listening and thinking that goes into community development work to respond to victims of a natural disaster or a civil conflict should have happened well before the crisis was at hand. In the case of a genuine emergency, listening and thinking may be abbreviated, or done in tandem with community action.

But in work that is not crisis management, lasting impact rarely happens through quick actions and impulsive decision making. In their analysis of what causes unethical behavior in public administration work, two Italian professors note time pressure as a key factor in driving unethical behavior (Belle & Cantarelli, 2017). No, lasting impact happens when we roll up our sleeves, get our hands dirty, show patience, and do the listening and thinking first. Good community development work is a long game and results often come slowly. Strong relationships require conversations, discussions, and community processes that all take time. You can expedite the process, but not without sacrificing quality. We have seen first-hand community development work in the United States and in Uganda where the intended successes were never achieved, and with each case we would suspect that something was missed in the listening and thinking phases. Sometimes these phases have been overlooked altogether.

Even if you are in the enviable position of having all the time and resources in the world to conduct your community conversations, it can be extremely difficult to create a truly equitable space; a space that gives people from different geographies, cultures, and socioeconomic backgrounds a chance to be fully heard on issues that are integral to their livelihoods.

Developing a deep understanding of the context where you are working is a critical component of the thinking stage, and it can be a complicated undertaking. Whether you are dealing in international work across nations, or in domestic work across cities or towns, knowing the full context of a certain community is everything. Context can be molded by religion, gender, professional sector, or even by music and food. It is vital to interrogate and embrace the context in which we are doing our community development work, particularly when we were not born in the same communities where the work is being done. Skipping this process or cutting corners can have a devastating impact on your actions, anticipated goals, and objectives.

Back to the continent of Africa, where a history of conflict between cultures plays a crucial role in influencing the continent's collective development. As community development workers, we have been hit with this reality in countless ways during our collective decades of living and working in Uganda. For any community development work that is based on the African continent, historical context is impossible to avoid and foolish to ignore.

While we have studied the historical context of European colonialism in Africa extensively, we nevertheless learn new things each day, as history is ever evolving. As authors, we believe in a historical narrative that seeks to amend or shed light on potentially inaccurate views of past events. The approach our global education system takes to teaching about colonialism on the African continent needs to be revisited and updated to reflect historical facts that have been uncovered over time through careful research and analysis. The historical evidence available to us today is more precise and accurate than, say, in 1968 when Ivan Illich was making his own assertions. We believe that historians also must listen, think, and act, and that new information uncovered should better inform our collective understanding of communities around the globe.

Europe's invasive overhaul of our world's second largest continent has left lasting impacts and continued ripple effects in communities all around Africa that have direct implications for the community development work we discuss. We firmly believe that a more honest and unbiased historical account of colonialism in Africa should be taught in classrooms around the globe if we are going to change the way that people perceive and engage with countries in this region. The significance of colonialism and its manipulative and inhumane practices should be exposed in our classrooms and in our textbooks if we are to find our way forward together in advancing a more collective and collaborative approach to community development anywhere in formerly colonized regions. This realization has given rise to important new fields and modes of study, such as postcolonial studies and decoloniality. Interested students will find fascinating perspectives by exploring these emerging academic disciplines.

What happens when this contextual history is ignored? In Uganda, we see first-hand community development efforts driven by external groups go awry due to a lack of empathy and understanding of the local population and culture. This theme plagues community development organizations and practitioners who have not listened, have not taken the time to exchange ideas, and have not engaged in the important conversations about societal issues at hand. In his book *States and Powers in Africa*, Jeffrey Herbst offers perspectives on the impact that colonialism had on the entire continent of Africa, and the subservience and arbitrary approach Westerners took to forcing their values and cultures onto the people they colonized (Herbst, 2014). Community development practitioners who do not understand this disconnect not only repeat some of the same mistakes, but also do incalculable damage by reinforcing norms that disempower and create dependence among historically excluded communities. Historical context should drive the way in which development organizations communicate with local populations. Awareness of the Holocaust informs collective understanding of the Jewish people. An awareness of the atrocities that Pol Pot committed in Cambodia is relevant to how development organizations engage and communicate with people in Cambodia. Lack of historical context leaves the practitioner at high risk of making serious miscalculations in their community development work.

This disconnect is what has led, in large part, to what can best be described as "neo-colonialism." And when we are not careful, the NGO industry in the developing world can serve as the inadvertent extension of colonialism in the communities where philanthropic-minded visitors operate.

Neo-colonialism is a term that was coined by Kwame Nkrumah in the 1960s to describe the ways in which world powers engaged with the newly formed independent nations of Africa that had formerly been colonized (Nkrumah, 2009). Nkrumah was Ghana's first president and arguably one of Africa's most influential political leaders over the past century. In Africa, neo-colonialism is essentially a continuation of colonialism masked as a collective effort by foreign nations and organizations to help local communities to achieve freedom and development. After African nations gained independence from colonial rule, they still had to rely heavily on their former imperial powers for security and aid. This further deepened international power dynamics that persist across the continent today (Nnamdi, 2016).

Nkrumah's framework for understanding this relationship is helpful in unpacking international community development practices that are inadvertently harmful. But this reality is not specific to Africa alone. The same ideas and issues that Nkrumah helped popularize retain their relevance all around the world in community development work—even in domestic contexts.

That is why having these important and often difficult conversations is so critical to the collective work. If you belong to a Western organization coming to Uganda to engage in community development work, you need to investigate and understand the role that NGOs have served in that area over the past few decades. You need to talk honestly about what did not go well. You should talk about neo-colonialism, and you should think critically about terms like "voluntourism" and "philanthro-tourism," and the impact such activities have on the communities where they take place. You might even revisit Illich when you witness cases where good intentions result in doing more harm than good. As you are thinking about the communities where you are working, ask yourself what the intentions are of the NGOs who have served and are serving this community.

While exchanging ideas with communities and doing your best thinking, consider examples of each of these processes in your own work and/or academic experiences. The misguided approach to community development—where we do not factor in the context, history, and power dynamics of a region—does not just happen when Americans try to work in Africa or Asia or South America and forget to listen and think. It also happens when people from Kenya and Uganda try to engage in this work in the slums of Nairobi and Kampala; and it happens when people in the United States do this work with underserved communities in Baltimore, Maryland, or Salt Lake City, Utah. Where you are from or how good your intentions are don't matter when it comes to good community development; what matters is how you listen and think in the community development work you do, regardless of where you do it.

Without oversimplifying, the remedy for the misguided development approach can be relatively simple: take time to get to know and understand the history of the community. Study the community's history, watch their films, and read books written by local authors. We see countless volunteers and community workers who arrive in Uganda who do not know who the president is, the population, or even what the capital city is. These visitors have not taken the time to understand the many different languages spoken, the complexities of the tribes, or even which country colonized and influenced the people in the region.

Imagine going to a new doctor to get treated for something serious, and in your first consult she does not ask you any questions, but rather immediately offers you a prescription or begins a procedure. There is no effort to acquire family history or information about symptoms or causes. Now, imagine going to a country to help with something serious like public health or education and not asking any questions or understanding the community. Historical context is an antidote to combatting much of the neo-colonialism that occurs in Uganda and around the globe.

The Dynamic and Complicated Foreign Aid Conversation

Resources are a critical part of implementation, and most community development work cannot happen without them. Foreign aid is a formidable vehicle that wealthy nations use to assist other regions with various development challenges. These challenges in less developed communities and nations are familiar and consistent: poverty, wealth disparity, emerging markets, environmental degradation, gender inequity, poor public health, underfunded education infrastructure, lack of employment opportunities, religious intolerance, and many others.

All these issues need to be addressed in the context of larger global trends that are similarly complex. Donor–recipient relationships are much different than a generation ago. Climate change promises both foreseeable and unforeseeable impacts. Economic globalization has augmented and complicated the interdependence between nations. However, there are some common myths our world has about these familiar issues, which paint an unnecessarily negative picture of existing efforts and stand in the way of progress.

In their 2014 Annual Letter, Bill and Melinda Gates outline three of these common myths heard about the world's poor (Gates, 2014):

1. Poor countries are doomed to stay poor.
2. Foreign aid is a waste.
3. Saving lives leads to overpopulation.

These myths grow as they become perceived as facts by the general population, with no consideration of data or science to support the original claims.

1. The first myth leads to acceptance of "the way things are" and discourages changemakers from addressing poverty issues that may be preventable.

2. Consider the second myth: if millions of people in the United States believe that foreign aid is a waste, then that will put huge pressure on policy makers to consider reducing the nation's pivotal budget for international foreign aid.
3. Finally, the third myth is not only unfounded from a demographic perspective, but implies that certain communities' lives are more or less important than others.

Over the past ten years, African nations have had 27 leadership changes, contributing to a rise in democracy as well as an effort to improve transparency, accountability, and rule of law (Signé et al., 2019). The rise of social media is credited as a catalyst for major world events like the Arab Spring and allows ideas to flow more quickly and freely than in generations past (Howard et al., 2011). Democracy is still imperiled on the African continent due to the corruption of leaders in power, alongside the difficulty of institutionalizing secure changes in leadership through legitimate processes (National Research Council, 1992), but overall indicators of health and prosperity are improving (Brien, 2020). In addition, African nations have made huge improvements to their public health systems, resulting in a substantial decline in maternal and child deaths as well as progress in preventing childhood illnesses and communicable diseases (Signé et al., 2019). Uganda has seen a rise in life expectancy at birth, a rise in GDP per capita, and a decline in the percentage of the population living in poverty, all within the past few years (World Bank: Uganda, 2020). Neighboring Rwanda has seen marked improvements and similar growth as well, alongside increases in primary school attendance, adult literacy rate, and gender equality indices (Newey, 2019).

Despite false narratives about the world's poor, a key player in international development funding is not saying that our collective work is done, or even close to it. There is a lot more to do, and some poor countries have stayed poor. For instance, Mali is still struggling to recover from their Ebola crisis in 2014-2016 (Giovetti, 2019). Primary school enrollment has dropped since 2011 and 41% of the population is living under the poverty line, with an average life expectancy of 58 years (World Bank: Mali, 2020). Other African countries like Niger, Sierra Leone, and Burundi are also still struggling to escape their classification as "poor" (Giovetti, 2019).

This again provides cause for question about foreign aid's effectiveness. In the 21st century, the world is paying closer attention to the development of African countries than ever before. Thirty-two percent of aid from the United States is allocated to nations in Africa, the most of any region (McBride,

2018). Demographic shifts in China have caused multinational corporations to look for a new and younger labor force, creating more opportunities for expatriate employees who are commonly migrating towards the African continent (Myers et al., 2019). Technology is creating a world where game-changing new apps and ideas can come from anywhere – not just from "developed" countries or famous centers of entrepreneurship such as Silicon Valley (Muroyama & Guyford 1988). Mobile banking has become one of Africa's best-known accomplishments, allowing people to save money by avoiding banking fees (Shapshak, 2015). Bank Zero Mutual Fund, Discovery Bank, and Shyft are just a few of the prosperous apps created in African countries that have made a lasting impression around the world (Shapshak, 2015). Kenya has become a global tech hub and is creating innovations that the United States and other nations use to inform their decisions (Ream, 2019). In 2018, 50% of Kenya's GDP was associated with M-Pesa, a mobile banking application created locally (Shapshak, 2015).

With so much foreign aid coming into African countries, how is this widespread developmental stagnancy possible? Our society also needs to be wary of the fact that foreign aid and engagement has the potential to create enormous dependencies and foster corruption. Millions of dollars meant to trickle down to the poorest recipient communities end up in pockets of corrupt politicians or are directed into programs with enormous salary and overhead costs that cannot sustain themselves long enough to create lasting positive change. This helps explain why myths about the ineffectiveness of foreign aid exist! Increased accountability and improved methodology in distributing aid is paramount to sustainable development of target communities.

Taken together, these considerations make foreign aid an even more challenging undertaking than it was just a decade ago. These factors also make us increasingly aware of how interconnected we all are in this globalized world. With a finite pool of resources and increasingly complex social issues in the areas of education, health care, conservation, and public management of resources, a healthy discourse and exchange of ideas is required to better understand the roles of various actors and change agents—government, private sector, nonprofit organizations, and foundations—and how communities can most effectively address the global infrastructure challenges faced in both urban centers and rural communities.

We need to talk about this collaboratively, across nations and backgrounds, in a way that is critical and honest. Clearly, some efforts to intervene have not worked despite best intentions. The impetus is on us as community development leaders to talk about why this is, exchange ideas, and figure it out. How can the development world do better?

Foreign aid and community engagement can be enormously helpful in low-income countries when successfully managed, effectively distributed to local systems, and informed by the needs of the communities for which the support is intended.

> *Additional Learning:* If you want to see how well you know the world in terms of international development and health data, check out GapMinder. org to take the Gapminder Test, explore Dollar Street, and review their easy-to-use database!

A Growing Need for Idea Exchange

Hopefully we have made our point clear: the importance of having critical conversations about community issues cannot be overstated. Here is a problem you may run into during your work. It's safe to assume that the stakeholders best positioned to determine their needs are those individuals in the community directly affected by a problem. We could be talking about weather patterns that cause agricultural irregularities leading to season-to-season intermittent poverty among farmers, or a stigmatization of homosexuality that ostracizes young people in LGBTQ communities.

But what happens if a target community may not know exactly what innovations and services would solve their problems? As we have said, many problems in community development are not simple, and will not just disappear with a simple intervention or a hasty donation. Deep-rooted behavior has the immobility of a lethargic elephant. It's not going anywhere anytime soon. These complexities create a legitimate opportunity for constructive idea exchange between direct stakeholders and community development practitioners. And while we need to always engage the community in the work that we do as collaborators and partners, we also know there are ideas and resources we can bring to the table that can help these communities thrive. Sister Jovita was not opposed to Jamie bringing her new medical supplies; she simply wanted to do it in partnership and collaboration with him so her insights could better inform and guide the efforts!

What might this exchange look like in practice? What if we try to encourage young people in our communities to get involved in these critical conversations? While listening and thinking is important for us to do in our community development work, such efforts cannot be successful if the people who live in the communities do not reciprocate. Let us travel down to a crater lake in the southwestern corner of Uganda and look at one example of what idea exchange and cross-cultural conversations can look like. Before we start, consider this question: "if you could have a conversation with someone from the other side of the world about an issue that is important to you, what would you want to tell them that you think they should know?"

––––––––

"Millennial Exchange of Ideas: A Lakeside Leadership Summit," by: Thomas Karrel

During the last weekend of June 2019, I found myself back in southwestern Uganda for another visit to Lake Bunyonyi. Before I visited, I had many assumptions about Uganda's landscape, and Lake Bunyonyi challenged them all. This crater lake, rumored to be the second deepest in Africa, resembles an oil painting brought to life. You find yourself surrounded by towering hills on all sides, spotted with small farms and the homes of thousands of Ugandan families who call Bunyonyi home. The area is brought to life each day by the nonstop singing of over 200 different bird species. In the mornings and evenings, the lake resembles a glass floor, punctuated by the dozens of islands spread across the surface.

At one point, I sat with my feet dangling off a wooden dock on the edge of a small peninsula, jutting out in the water. Only accessible by boat or footpaths, this peninsula is home to Entusi Resort and Retreat Center, a unique destination for travelers, students, and community leaders from around the globe. That place truly embodies the meaning of a "community-run" initiative. Entusi opened in 2012 and was built by over 150 local community members to create a space to serve as a world-class destination for travelers, a place where people who live nearby could gather to discuss community challenges with prospective donors, and a facility that employs dozens of local workers while aiming to positively impact the health and vitality of the local community.

What made that weekend so special was not only that I was sitting on a dock at Entusi, but that I was sharing the peninsula with close to 76 people from around the globe. Entusi's 26 staff members, all Ugandan and born in the area, set the stage for me and 49 other students and educators from the United States, Uganda, Rwanda, and the Democratic Republic of Congo to connect, exchange ideas and think critically about community development together. This was the first evening of a three-day youth leadership summit that would bring together high school students from completely different corners of the

Earth and from diverse socioeconomic, cultural, and religious backgrounds. Together we would push past our preconceptions and boundaries to have conversations with one another about the most important issues we face in our modern society.

That weekend, the small peninsula transformed into a microcosm of our world, where a student from Sacramento, California could connect with a student from Gashora, Rwanda about gender imbalances in their schools. A student from a low-income corner of New Orleans, Louisiana could learn alongside a Congolese student from the Kyangwali Refugee Settlement about what poverty means and how to overcome economic disadvantages. You get the idea.

During that first Friday evening, I found myself standing in front of all these different people, their eyes glowing from the pure excitement of the environment in which we found ourselves. One of the students said it perfectly that first evening: "the opportunity to exchange experiences and challenge ideas across cultures and backgrounds is invaluable, whether as a youth or an adult. It can truly change the way we view our world, and our own community."

What we tend to forget is that each individual person on this planet, around 7.8 billion people last time I checked, has their own unique experiences and insights that deserve to be shared. Everyone has knowledge that can translate into valuable solutions to solve key problems that inhibit a given community. But too often we do not give each other that chance to exchange ideas, think critically, and create actionable items on how to bring those theories to life.

This is where the magic happens. If you give young, motivated people an opportunity to tell their stories, critically discuss the problems they face, and exchange ideas on how to address those issues, something amazing can happen. You watch those students transform into the next generation of leaders. You see them grow into people who are more than capable of steering our global community into a phase of greater equity and empowerment.

I run the youth summit to follow the Listen. Think. Act. approach. The listening phase is all about listening and sharing stories, developing common understanding, while the think phase is all about listening and sharing ideas, ideally ones that are actionable and promote further discussion. Then, the act phase is where we figure out what ideas need to come to life, and how these students will take them back to their various communities. No one is left behind, and each person is fully engaged in the idea exchange.

On that peninsula, as June rolled into July, we sat around in circles, discussing how climate change was impacting our lifestyles, and how racial and economic inequities were inhibiting young people from seeking higher education. We learned what it meant to grow up living in a refugee settlement in an entirely different country from the one in which you were born, and what it felt like to have a leader who undermined your community and your own self-worth. We learned what issues plague communities on the south side of Chicago in the central part of the United States, and what problems citizens in the remote region of Karamoja face in Northern Uganda.

One specific exchange was two groups of students from Chicago and Kampala. These students were challenged to identify the top inhibitors to their community's development, and came up with racism and education access, respectively. All students were pushed to hear out the other stories about why these issues posed such a significant challenge and helped to brainstorm ideas and possible solutions to both racism in Chicago and education access in Kampala. In fact, upon reflection, many students shared several "lightning bolt moments" from hearing ideas posed by the group from a different country. The students from Kampala were helping the Chicago students see racism from a new perspective. This resulted in ideas that the students believed they "never would have thought of without this unique exchange".

Young people will change our world. Over that weekend, my few remaining doubts about that truth faded away. Youth leaders can be the key that brings about good community development work, but they need the space to exchange ideas, be creative, and think out loud together.

That weekend I witnessed first-hand how bringing together talented people from different backgrounds and geographical areas creates a truly one-of-a-kind environment. All those young men and women are highly capable leaders, whether they know it or not, and they each have the potential to create sustainable change in their own communities across the globe, as well as to work together to solve our world's most pressing and complicated issues. That collective potential is simply amplified by an idea exchange like the one we shared on Lake Bunyonyi.

———

To augment this story, let's dig a little deeper here. Listening is all about taking time to learn, absorb, engage, and share stories. Thinking is all about sharing ideas. We want to specify how collective idea-sharing, analysis, and decision-making should work. Take, for instance, a group of high school students from the Denver School of Science and Technology who visited Akagera National Park in 2017, just as Rwanda was reopening the area. The warden discussed with the students the challenges that his team was encountering with poachers, and the limited capacity to patrol the park. After a long time listening, thinking, and exchanging ideas with the park warden, the students responded by building him a drone that directly addressed his needs. The story was featured in the New York Times and the students were invited to the home of Paul Kagame, the President of Rwanda, to demonstrate how the drone worked.

These stories emphasize the need for idea exchange and offer specific examples of what this practice looks like in a cross-cultural setting. Such examples illustrate people practicing good community development by thinking together, finding common ground, identifying obstacles, understanding historical context, and making an action plan to move forward. From here we will move on to discuss how to exchange good ideas.

A Simple Approach to Idea Exchange

When we jump into an idea exchange in our community development work, we like to use this simple framework as a starting point. Seek answers to these three questions from your users and their target communities (Johnson, 2020):

1. What do you want for your community? *(Goals)*
2. What is standing in the way of this? *(Limitations)*
3. What can you do to remove these limitations and achieve your community goals? *(Action Items)*

Obviously, this is a very stripped-down and simplified approach to idea exchange. But start here and realize that these questions can grow in complexity according to the context in which you are working. As we described in Chapter One, when you give people a legitimate seat at the table and ask them to share their stories and be candid, then they will be much more open to brainstorm and exchange ideas on potential solutions to their problems. What you may find in practice is that their feedback is much deeper and richer in possibilities than the feedback would have been without a proper idea exchange and a balanced conversation in which all participants have a voice.

More than anything else, the single most important part of exchanging ideas is ensuring that the actual users being impacted by a given problem are leading the conversations. Community development dialogues and thinking processes need to include local stakeholders. If you are working in Chicago, or in Kigali, plan your conversations accordingly. Do not underestimate the complexity of this process. Increasingly, various development leaders and students enter community work with some intention to listen and think with local stakeholders. However, it is much more common that these groups believe they are listening and thinking together with local community members, when in fact there are various disconnects and gaps in information.

This was touched on in Chapter One with Denver's Road Home, but it is important to dig a little deeper here. Thinking will be shortchanged if organizations presume that only "official" people with "official" roles are those who need to be engaged and invited to the discussion table. There are many layers to stakeholder engagement. Youth, residents, local volunteers, and other members of the community all have a lot to contribute, if provided the right opportunity.

As the community development industry's desire to solve community challenges speeds up through technology and the demands and expectations of funders, we believe that it is increasingly rare that community development workers engage in this thinking process with any degree of thoroughness. In many cases, it is much more common that practitioners believe they are listening and thinking together, when in fact they are not.

Why are these conversations so vital? Let us revisit a question posed earlier. What happens if a community is aware of the problems they face, but is not familiar with existing solutions that are helping to mitigate similar problems in other parts of the world? And for further consideration, maybe there are new solutions about to be discovered that will follow simply from assembling the right minds at the same table.

A great example of this potential knowledge gap can be seen in the global agricultural sector, where many farmers face the impacts of climate change. Consider a rural, agrarian community in Lira, Northern Uganda, as a focus community. The farmers in Lira undoubtedly know their land better than anyone else on the planet. Their families have lived and farmed in those communities for generations, and consequently these farmers spend most of their lives focused on the intersection of agriculture and weather. However, fluctuations in our planet's climate are causing increased irregularities in weather patterns for farmers around the world and reducing agricultural productivity (Environmental Protection Agency, 2016). If you are a farmer in Northern Uganda, one of the countries situated on the equator, it is harder than ever to anticipate and follow the semi-annual rainy seasons in your region. Additionally, studies have shown that countries closer to the equator are facing droughts and increased temperatures, causing worse living and working conditions (McKenna, 2020). If you can create a space for climate experts to connect with these farmers, it is possible that some positive community transformation can happen. But to create a viable solution, it cannot just work on paper or in a textbook. These interactions must lead to a back-and-forth exchange of ideas as the participants on both sides really dig into both the potential solutions and anticipated challenges. Ultimately, for such efforts to succeed, the idea exchange must have farmer input and buy-in at its very core.

In some cases, the listening phase, even when it is characterized by extensive community research, can still turn out to be limited in terms of results if your identified problem has no existing solutions in place. The target community always has the most knowledge of their situation, but what happens if they might not know exactly what innovations and services they need? Or what is even feasible? In some cases, the community members you have been listening to and communicating with may have no frame of reference for what a solution to their problem would even look like.

This brings us to a concept coined by Dorothy Leonard and Jeffrey Rayport in a 1997 *Harvard Business Review* article: "Empathic Design". As discussed in their article,

> "...the techniques of empathic design–gathering, analyzing, and applying information gleaned from observation in the field– are familiar to top engineering/design companies and to a few forward-thinking businesses, but they are not common practice" in the field of community development (Leonard & Rayport, 2014).

At the foundation of empathic design is observation: watching and experiencing the problems various community members face, and how they come up with or engage different solutions. Observation is best conducted in the user's own environment, during normal, everyday routines. Focus on creating conversations and spaces for idea exchange where users have the full ability to be heard, describe their problems, and interact with questions posed by community development organizations who want to offer solutions. These conversations happen best when informed by relationship-building, which we will turn to in our next chapter.

"The Art of Community Organizing through Collaborative Thinking,"
by: Agnes Igoye

One of the most important classes I ever took was in 2011. I was a Fulbright Hubert H. Humphrey Fellow at the University of Minnesota, and my area of specialization was the prevention of human trafficking. The course was all about 'community organizing' and it was titled "Organizing for the Public Good". I learned from the best, benefiting from the teachings and mentorship of Professors Harry C. Boyte and Dennis Donovan.

In the 1960's, Boyte worked for Dr. Martin Luther King Jr. as a field secretary in the civil rights movement. Later he became the national coordinator of the New Citizenship (1993-1995), a broad non-partisan effort to bridge the citizen–government gap. He presented findings to President Clinton and Vice President Gore at a 1995 Camp David seminar on the future of democracy, helping shape Clinton's 'New Covenant' State of the Union that year (University of Minnesota, 2021). Dennis Donovan is the national organizer of Public Achievement at the Sabo Center for Democracy and Citizenship at Augsburg University in Minneapolis, Minnesota. Working together, Donovan and Boyte collaborated to develop Public Achievement, a pioneering citizen education initiative (University of Minnesota, 2021). Basically, these guys were the real deal, and I wanted to absorb as much insight as I could from their experiences.

In their course, I was introduced to key concepts surrounding civic agency, as well as countless organizing skills like conducting one-on-one relational meetings, power mapping, collective problem solving, and public speaking. I got to understand the importance of my own public narrative and the stories of others and how that can lead to a new level of awareness about the necessity to act. I came to better understand and use power, form partnerships across lines of difference, understand diverse self-interests, and recognize the importance of knowing the culture, history, and social networks of places that are critical in international/community development work (Donovan, 2015).

As I immersed myself in the community organizing teachings of Professors Boyte and Donovan, I interacted with many American students who thought human trafficking only happened in developing countries. Then suddenly, one cold afternoon as I was homesick, missing the glorious Ugandan sunshine, I came across a Somali immigrant community web page with reports of a trafficking ring. Somali girls from Minnesota had been trafficked as far as the state of Tennessee (Forliti, 2011). I reached out to one of Minnesota's migrant community leaders, Somali Activist Abdirizak Bihi. Years prior, while I was home in Uganda, I remembered watching Bihi speak on Al Jazeera following the death of his 18-year-old nephew Burhan Hassan in 2009. His nephew was one of many young Somali men who went missing from Minneapolis, after being recruited by radical elements to fight in Somalia, where he was ultimately killed (The Associated Press, 2009).

Meeting Bihi was formative for me. I had the chance to employ my newly acquired community organizing skills during a one-on-one meeting with a leader who knew his community better than anyone. In preparation, I conducted a 30-minute conversation with Professor Boyte. My questions zeroed in on what led him, a White male, to join the civil rights movement. As a young boy, he could not comprehend the idea that he could not play with his best friend, just because he was Black. This was his story of self, what connected him to the stories of others–building blocks to the civil rights movement. This conversation helped me shape my own story of displacement and fleeing the Lord's Resistance Army, and why I dedicated my life to counter human trafficking.

———

For our readers who want a little more guidance and direction about how to engage in collaborative thinking, we have offered some recommended readings at the end of the chapter that will allow you to dig deeper. For the purposes of this text, we want to make sure you leave this chapter recognizing how important this technique is to master, and there are other texts that do a far better job of teaching and honing this skill.

Let us now look at how the community development principle of Bihi, a Somali immigrant, can guide and inform a community in Minnesota.

———

"Cross-Cultural Learning in Action: From Somalia to Minneapolis,"
by: Agnes Igoye

In a similar vein, Bihi's activism came to prominence after the death of his nephew in Somalia. He never considered that his wonderful and brilliant nephew could be radicalized to go and fight in Somalia. Bihi was determined to keep his community safe from organized crime. This initial interaction connected me in a deep way to Bihi, a brilliant community organizer. He then introduced me to members of his community, the Somali diaspora, and particularly to the parents and the youth who were primarily targeted by human traffickers. With two of my classmates, we conducted one-on-one interviews with these youth, women, and men. We held community dialogues to establish the causes and dynamics of human trafficking in the Somali communities in Minneapolis, Minnesota.

The outcomes were astonishing! It was a case of integration gone wrong. Speaking with the young people provided them a more honest space, and they complained of how strict their parents were. "Our parents do not want us to adopt the American ways," they told us. The parents wanted their children to retain their Somali traditions. Dress, socialize, and speak Somali. The parents confirmed this, one mother acknowledging that "[she could] never let [her] children speak to [her] in English. In [our] household, only our mother tongue of Somali will be spoken."

This created a fertile recruiting ground for traffickers. They targeted teens who felt alienated from their parents and wanted to rebel against the strict rules they faced at home and promised to help them escape. The traffickers would pose as saviors and boyfriends, offering love and freedom. The end game was to initiate these run-away children into sexual exploitation.

However, after a lot of listening and thinking together as a community, the affected Somali families decided to act. The parents understood the importance and advantage of speaking English to enable integration into their new home. The teenagers equally understood the importance of learning and preserving their Somali language and culture, staying connected to their roots.

This experience motivated me to attend Minnesota State task force meetings. Big shout out to Richard Wexler, the state coordinator for *Not for Sale* in Minnesota at the time. Not only did he introduce me to the task force, where my views and perspectives were welcomed, but he also encouraged me to attend "The Not for Sale Academy" in San Francisco. At the Academy, they assembled a team of trainers from government, civil society, and academia. The academy taught me so much about the difficult job of being a human trafficking investigator, through hearing from officers at San Jose Police Department and the FBI. At some point, I had to acknowledge my own shortcomings and come to the realization that investigating online sexual exploitation of children was not my calling. I could not look at the graphic images and videos of adults exploiting children! I excused myself from that training session. I learned a fundamental lesson in the process, which was to have the humility to accept that I cannot do everything. Teamwork and collaboration matter.

Later I found a home at *The Women's Foundation of Minnesota* under the visionary leadership of Lee Roper-Batker. While doing an internship there, I was honored to be part of the team that helped launch the "Minnesota Girls Are Not for Sale" campaign in 2011, a $7.5 million cross-sector campaign to end sex-trafficking. The campaign resulted in substantial change to Minnesota's response on this issue and leveraged a $27 million state investment (Day, 2019). Years later, to bring the relationship full circle, we hosted a team from *The Women's Foundation of Minnesota* in Uganda, which inspired leaders of that organization to support our human trafficking survivor rehabilitation programs at the Dream Revival Center in Uganda (University of Minnesota, 2018).

Community organizing classes, fieldwork, and attending the dynamic Minnesota State counter-trafficking task force meetings for a whole year taught me lessons that informed the creation of our own task force after I returned to Kampala. Those idea exchanges about what was happening in the United States shaped my community work in Uganda. The people you meet and the ideas you share are instrumental in doing community development work, wherever in the world you are.

During my fellowship in Minnesota, I will never forget how I kept in constant touch with my colleagues back in Uganda. I updated them about my experiences and consulted them on lessons I should seek out that would be useful to our environment back home. At the same time, I also kept in touch with colleagues who were making strides in the counter-trafficking field. So often, some professionals have a difficult time reintegrating into their workplaces upon return from studies abroad. The challenge partly stems from the fact that when one disappears for say one year or more, the lives of the people one leaves behind do not remain static. When you do not keep in touch, you may succumb to an assumption that you have superior knowledge and skills because of your time abroad. You will return home and find that your colleagues have equally advanced at their work. Have the humility to know that they, too, will have something to teach you.

It has become a habit of mine, upon return from studies abroad, to listen more. I always get comments from colleagues such as "Agnes became quieter when she went to America". It is my strategy of ensuring that I listen more than I speak, to learn about and catch up with the progress of my colleagues during my absence. Listening also helps to evaluate what lessons would be useful to share from my overseas education. Sometimes you may return with knowledge that you assume is new and yet your colleagues have moved a step further than you! Funny how that goes.

I always try to seek ways to set up exchanges of ideas with various people in my life, to help think critically about all this new information in my mind, as well as theirs. These idea exchanges are what transform insights into strategies, and stories into action.

––––––––

Ultimately the stories in this chapter demonstrate the synergies between listening and thinking, where idea exchange is influenced by the historical and cultural context of the communities being served. When done well, these ideas can move and translate from the horn of Africa to the Great Lakes region of the Midwestern United States.

Summing Up

There is enormous power in exchanging ideas across communities, cultures, and countries. In practice, having these critical conversations around societal issues is not easy, and doing it well creates a crucial foundation for good community development work. This applies to world leaders at annual UN conferences, and it applies to community development workers in communities around the world, in the last mile of development work.

We have discussed the power of critical conversations and idea exchange from multiple perspectives and have emphasized the importance of grasping the overarching historical context in community development work. Concrete examples of foreign aid gone bad, and the impact of neo-colonial thinking may also be critical to understanding the more immediate context of a specific focus area. These are all key prisms to consider when exchanging ideas in the community development process. Ultimately, this step of effective idea exchange sets the stage for our next chapter, where we will see how strong, lasting relationships and truly collaborative partnerships between stakeholders will ultimately define how sustainable and effective your community development work is over time.

––––––––

CHAPTER THREE "COMMUNITY CHANGEMAKER" CHALLENGE:
DEFINE

By this point, you have been able to push your comfort zone a bit, and dive into a stage of empathy building and discovery about your area of interest that has hopefully given you a clearer sense of the specific experiences and issues that your user(s) faces. Let us define what those are.

- Based on your research up to this point, identify a specific experience within this area of interest faced by your user(s). Ask yourself: "what is a specific challenging experience had by the user in your community that you wish to address?"
  - Example: within the New Orleans East community, the area of interest is mental health, and the user—a teenage boy—struggles to find people who will listen to his problems from an unbiased, anonymous viewpoint without fear of his parents hearing, and needs a way to fully express his emotions and weaknesses.
- Discuss your experience definition statement with a colleague or friend and create an idea exchange of your own. Focus on what comes to mind after reading your statement. Reread it a couple of times and, with your colleague, brainstorm a list of words, ideas, insights, and drawings to start bringing it to life.

Your aim in this phase is to challenge yourself to go deep. Do not necessarily go for the first thing that pops into your head. Take some time to consider all facets of this person's experience. Use the idea exchange to bring out new considerations, questions, and insights that you may have been overlooking. What is at the root of your user's dilemma?

Chapter Three Conversation Starters

- What aspects of the discourse around international development and NGOs can be challenged?
- Which dynamics or themes about international development are more difficult to point out or challenge?
- How do you feel about the concept of "neo-colonialism"?
- What similar subjects to neo-colonialism, if any, did you cover in your education?
- Think about the last conversation you have had with people from different communities/backgrounds:
  - How would you describe this experience?
  - What was the biggest challenge of having this conversation?
  - What did you learn about yourself after this experience?
  - Why do you think effective idea exchange can be so difficult across different cultures and communities? (Assume there is no language barrier to contest with.)

- Take some time to reflect on the first half of this book with friends or colleagues.
  - How have the first three chapters of this book changed or shaped your views of community development work so far?
  - Which community perspective has stood out the most to you and why?

Chapter Three Additional Recommended Content

- Dambisa, M. (2009). Dead Aid: Why Aid Is Not Working and How There Is a Better Way for Africa. Farrar, Straus, and Giroux.
- Dearden, N. (2017, May 24). Africa is not poor, we are stealing its wealth. Business and Economy | Al Jazeera.
- Easterly, W. (2007). The White Man's Burden: Why the West's Efforts to Aid the Rest Have Done So Much Ill and So Little Good. Penguin Books.
- Gawande, A. (2013, July 22). Sharing Slow Ideas. The New Yorker.
- Nkrumah, K. (2009). Neo-Colonialism: The Last Stage of Imperialism. Panaf.
- Pinker, S. (2019). Enlightenment Now: The Case for Reason, Science, Humanism, and Progress. Penguin Books.
- Rosling, O. (2021). Gapminder. GapMinder Website. (Worldview Upgrader, Dollar Street, & Interactive Database)
- Rosling, H., Rönnlund, A. R., & Rosling, O. (2018). Factfulness: Ten Reasons We're Wrong About the World--and Why Things Are Better Than You Think. Flatiron Books.

CHAPTER FOUR
Forge Strong Relationships:
Partnering With Clear Intention

"Do not depend on the hope of results. When you are doing the sort of work you have taken on, you may have to face the fact that your work will be apparently worthless and even achieve no result at all, if not perhaps results opposite to what you expect. As you get used to this idea, you start to concentrate more and more not on the results but on the value, the rightness, the truth of the work itself. And there too a great deal has to be gone through, as gradually you struggle less and less for an idea and more and more for specific people. The range tends to narrow down, but it gets more real. In the end, it is the reality of personal relationships that saves everything."
- Thomas Merton, in a letter to Jim Forest dated February 21, 1966.

Thomas Merton was called "the monk who became a prophet" (Jacob et al., 2018). We often cite his writing in our lectures and courses. His words are simple, timeless, and very relevant to our approach to community development. Merton embraced the concepts of Listen. Think. Act. well before we came around. If we had only one paragraph to include in this chapter, we would remind you of the reference Merton makes to the collective work of human beings. He tells us not to place too much trust in the results; that the truth is really in the process of the work that we do, and it is the power of personal relationships that "saves everything" (Merton, 1966).

This chapter looks at some of the key skills you need to master in building relationships that are intended to deliver positive processes. We hope to broaden your conception of what counts as a skill. While you could argue that building relationships is a virtue, we believe that this is a skill that requires practice to become a better community development worker.

Expanding on the importance of storytelling that we touched on in Chapter One, and the role that empathy plays in shaping these relationships in Chapter Two, Chapter Four takes a closer look at what it means to develop critical community development practices through building meaningful and lasting partnerships. We look at how to ensure you are thinking out loud with the people you serve and at some of the skills that go into activating and engaging all those who have a seat at the table. We talk about the importance of authenticity in your relationship-building and the advantages of informing your work from the ground up. As you establish these relationships and better understand the needs of a specific community, we turn our attention in the final part of this chapter to the art of finding common ground and achieving consensus to strategically move the community's initiatives forward.

Relationship building through community collaboration requires less action, less dictating, and more story-sharing, listening, and thinking. Collaboration, like good community development, is hard. In essence, collaboration is a shared experience where both parties need to yield to find common ground (Cambridge Dictionary, 2021). In the world of community development, it is often viewed as easier and faster to just do it yourself, unfortunately.

As you build relationships, you need to create a seat at the table for everyone. People engage when they genuinely feel like they are part of something. We have found this to be true regardless of geographic location. Chapter One reminds us that after you set that table and engage community partners who bring different perspectives and agendas, your next step is to find common ground. You do this by focusing not on where you differ, but where you agree. And the way that you convince people to engage in such a process is through relationships that involve clear intentions.

This chapter will be your recipe book for building relationships designed to make a difference. As you read the sections outlined here, ask yourself the following questions:

1. Given your own values and cultural lens, how would this process look if you were to set this table in a culturally appropriate way in the community where you are working?

2. Who should be part of the discussions and what constituencies do they represent?
3. What are your intentions for this group?
4. What are the challenges you will face and how will you handle conflict when it inevitably arises?
5. And once everyone is seated, how will you find common ground?

The Truth in Good Community Development: The Results vs. The Work

We need to dissect Merton's assumptions a little more. We place a lot of trust in results. We judge performance in class by the grades given to essays or exams. In an application for a grant, the funder usually wants to know what you are going to accomplish with the funds you receive. What will your results be if you win this grant and how will you measure outcomes?

Numeric results are key, and we should measure and demonstrate what we have accomplished and be held accountable. If we get $1 million to build housing for the homeless, we should produce results that show how many units of housing we built. If we build two units of housing when we agreed to build 20, that is, and should be, a problem for our funder. But this is not the whole story. Merton says, sure, you can pay attention to the tangible results. But the real action and the real outcomes lie in the way you do the work, and that is harder to quantify. This argument rings true for us, over our collective decades of community development work.

In good community development work, there are countless things we do every day that we cannot measure but believe have substantial impact. It is difficult to capture in a spreadsheet the effect you have while mentoring a young person who is having a hard day. It is challenging to document the gifts you give to a community, and a community gives to you, when you do not build or fix anything but do spend time connecting and forming relationships with people who live there. How does an organization measure the lasting relationships its employees make that are rooted in equity and respect? And is there any credit for impact if you go into a community thinking people who live there need something, and after engaging in story-sharing, empathy-building, idea exchange, and relationship-building, you conclude that you do not need to do what you originally intended? While results do matter, this chapter is about relationships, and we argue that in conducting good community development work, relationships frequently matter more than metrics.

Relationships are everything in community development. While you may still fail with them in place, we believe that nothing can succeed without them.

Result-Busting and Relationship Building

As we have seen in Chapters One and Three, colonists have been acting without listening or thinking since they first started arriving in the various communities that make up the African continent. And they were particularly inept at cultivating lasting relationships. They acted by building towns, introducing new religions, and replacing local cultural norms with their own (Herbst, 2014). They did not build equitable relationships at all when they arrived, and instead imposed their values, traditions, and beliefs on people they had never met before in the hopes of creating trade opportunities and transforming African countries into subsidiaries of Europe. Their arrival was predicated on seeking out resources that would benefit their own communities and advancing their own beliefs absent consideration of the people they encountered. While there are many texts that explore this in greater depth, here we see some of the roots of inequity and racism take shape, which have grown over time into immense modern challenges inhibiting the development of communities everywhere.

In some respects, many international nonprofits are still doing that today. We discussed this reality in the first three chapters: various development organizations and independent groups ship old cell phones and outdated textbooks and bring unwanted housing supplies and used clothes to help communities in African nations. They assume that if a community appears poor and lacking basic needs like education, then they should immediately build a school. They bring laptops to communities that do not have electricity and bring dilapidated electronics to people that have no wherewithal to repair dysfunctional devices.

Not everything being shipped is tangible. Religious ideas, cultural assumptions, and values are also exported. While there is nothing wrong in sharing one's beliefs, there is something inherently destructive about importing them to replace ideas that appear foreign to the visitor yet are deeply tied to a given community's people and their respective ancestry. Someone who is hungry and in need of healthcare for their family will abandon their form of worship and pray to a White savior if you compel them to do so to receive necessary resources. But that is not community development. That is proselytization.

Shipping laptops to a school that has neither electricity nor a teacher who knows how to operate the technology is not an achievement; it is a waste. Instead, good community development hinges on building strong relationships, and this takes time. Forming these sorts of enduring relationships would, in many cases, help to avoid the mistakes that are being made in community development today. If you have a relationship with the teachers at the school that does not have electricity, you surely will not make an appeal for your donors to send laptops that need to be plugged in.

Relationships require that we all stand there and get to know the people who live in a community. Real exchange requires that we understand the culture and context of the community members and how they make decisions; how they function individually and as a group. These relationships take much longer than a two-week mission trip or a speedy school volunteer experience, and when we forgo the listening and thinking along with relationship building–when we don't just stand there but do something and act–we make some of our worst mistakes.

After engaging in two different missionary trips, freelance journalist Mariette Williams shared her perspective on how these trips often cause more harm than good. She writes that "mission trips can create more problems for those on the receiving end of [the] perceived generosity, and part of the solution is refraining from short term trips, unless [you are] a skilled professional" in a specific discipline (Williams, 2019).

As a student or professional engaging in a new community, as an intern, advisor, project manager, or volunteer, the first step in relationship-building is what we have taught in every chapter of this book thus far; simply stand there. Share a meal, attend a worship service, visit a workplace, shop at the market, go to a baptism or birthday party, spend time walking around and getting to know the people who live in a place. Taste and smell and touch the community where you are working if you truly want to build the relationships you will need to have in place to foster change and determine if change is even desired by the community itself.

In relationship-building, standing there can be quite uncomfortable as you face real-world problems and try to resist an urge to draw conclusions. Our minds may tell us, "I know what you need. I have studied community development and it doesn't take much to tell that this community needs clean water." And while that may be true, as one in three people globally do not have access to potable water, how you go about drawing this conclusion is the most important part of community development work (UNICEF, 2019). As a good community development practitioner, you will not merely become more comfortable standing there, but you will amass a laundry list of questions as you do. These can help get you started:

- How many people live in this community?
- What is the story of how this community came to be?
- Who are the primary decision makers in this community?
- What do people do here to make money?
- What do people do here for fun?
- What customs do they celebrate?
- What are the biggest challenges confronting the people who live here?
- What do people living in this community feel that they need more than anything else?
- Who else is working in this area to support the community?
- What are the values of people in this community and how do they align with my own?

Through genuine patience, listening, curiosity, and empathy, you begin to follow the advice of Merton, who says that forming these basic relationships will "save everything." If you really want to bring clean water to a group of people and you do not know who makes decisions for this community, then you have a problem. However, if you build a real relationship with that community's influential stakeholders, and you take time to better understand the root causes of the issues being faced, then you begin to engage in truly effective relationships. These relationships will be very helpful when you run into the challenges that you will undoubtedly encounter along the way. We will save the rest of that point for Chapter Five, when we turn our attention to failures.

Community development practitioners sometimes skip the relationship-building stage based on a misplaced faith in their own expertise and experience. Being on the lookout for our own blind spots, regardless of how long we have been doing this work, can help create new insights.

The international development industry often incentivizes well-intended organizations and people to do things in communities located in poor countries that wealthier nations would never agree to have done to their own residents. Remember that wildly hypothetical story with some semblance of truth we talked about in Chapter One? Remember, the group of well-intentioned Ugandans showing up to build a school in New Orleans because they learned that the test scores were low, and the school district needed help?

We hear stories all the time of people showing up in the developing world with hammers, nails, and other supplies only to learn that the communities they visit already have all these things, not to mention highly competent construction workers, engineers, and architects. Our minds jump to building physical structures where all too often that is the last thing we should be spending resources on, if the collective goal is to truly respond to the challenges a given community faces. As you embark in community development work, enjoy the process of standing there and asking a lot of questions. Get to know the people you want to support and build genuine relationships. It will save you a lot of time and it will bring more truth to your work. And in turn, your results will be far more effective than your original, less-informed notions.

Back to Seating the Table

Like our stories in Chapter One, as you start the process of building strong relationships, your next challenge is to find all of the various people in the community who should have a seat at the table. If the only people you bring into the conversation are those who agree with you or those with whom your relationships are entirely positive, then you will build a very successful community project until the opposition gets in your way. It's crucial to also find the people most likely to criticize you, least likely to buy in, and most likely to tell you what they think is wrong about your approach! Find your opposition and start building or rebuilding those relationships early on.

Your table should not be confined to only those who agree with you and who have similar backgrounds. You should not all think alike. Good community development insists on including those who disagree or who are not necessarily in alignment with what you are doing. As we saw in Chapter One about building the homeless commission in Denver, setting the table with people from multiple perspectives and backgrounds will be essential in truly understanding where your challenges are going to come from.

Community development is tough as it pushes us out of our comfort zone in so many ways. First you have to stand there and get to know people before you act. Then you have to seek out not only those people who are like-minded and eager to meet and collaborate, you have to find the people who do not want anything to do with you and find out why that is the case. This is contrary to what most of us would do in our personal lives. The idea of finding the person at an event who is most critical of us or with whom we disagree the most is counterintuitive. But in most cases, if you are doing good community development work, it makes all the sense in the world. Engaging with your critics, skeptics, and people from opposite sides of the metaphorical debate stage will determine how well you and your target community succeed with the programs you build together.

"The Great Grogan Listening Tour," by Jamie Van Leeuwen

My mentors get most of the credit for the work I do. They shaped my values and perspectives and approaches to community development. Each of them entered my life at a specific time for a specific reason. Barb Grogan arrived in my life right as I was developing the homeless plan for then-Mayor Hickenlooper. A master of the universe, Barb had just sold her very successful industrial contracting company to assume the role of full-time philanthropist and community leader. She was looking for a project, and just as we were launching Denver's Road Home, I was successful in coaxing this private sector titan into helping guide and drive this community initiative. We had a specific role for her to play. We needed her to help us raise $50 million to build over 3,000 units of housing and decrease chronic homelessness by 75% in five years.

While Barb agreed to all these wildly audacious terms and an annual income of $0, she was very clear that before we raised a single dollar or built a single unit of housing, we had some listening and thinking to do. And this was not only for the people who supported the initiative. She wanted to meet with the foundation leaders, business leaders, elected officials, and community leaders who thought what we were doing was just plain batshit crazy. So, we began what I affectionately refer to as "the Great Grogan Listening Tour," where meeting after meeting revealed inefficiencies in how local government communicated with funders and a lack of accountability and transparency surrounding fund allocations.

We learned about fractured collaborations and uninspired, disengaged approaches to community development. It is amazing what people will tell you when all you do is listen. We did not have a lot to say, and we were not there to defend or excuse mistakes of the past. We wanted to know everything, because with each comment, complaint, and concern we could then devise a remedy. Better that more accountable evaluation could come from a university or academic partner. More collaborative funding could come from a resource allocation committee that involved all the funders. A more inspired and engaged approach could be guided and driven by the mayor himself.

And along the way our critics, the people most skeptical that we could implement Denver's Road Home, became our greatest allies. The business community, instead of criticizing the lackluster approach to homelessness, defended the work that we were doing. The business leaders would show up at City Council meetings to argue on behalf of efforts to create and zone more affordable housing. They even hosted an annual event for the homeless at a downtown hotel that raised over $2 million over time to support our work.

This is not to say that we all agreed on everything we did as it related to homelessness. The tour did not silence our critics. What the Great Grogan Listening Tour did was open the lines of communication so we could sit down at the table and negotiate toward a common ground. By listening, we built relationships with our critics and facilitated idea-exchange that rendered far more positive and productive outcomes than if we had launched an initiative devoid of input from our biggest critics.

———

There is a core lesson here: lean into the work by creating a seat at the table for your harshest critics and be willing to listen to them. You might not always agree, but the lines of communication that you open will serve you immensely over time.

For the aspiring public health worker ready to engage in a particular community, it is of course essential to find the community leaders who are accepting of the offer to help and partner. But in building relationships and understanding the context of the community at large, the outside public health worker should also look for the existing nonprofit organization(s) that insist they are already handling public health issues for the community and do not require any additional support. Or the traditional healer who dismisses any public health intervention under the premise that HIV is a "Western disease" and that someone who has AIDS has been cursed and should be dismissed and shamed by the community. That is the person the public health worker needs to engage.

As you tackle the exercise of seating your table, there are some important questions to ask. Some of these questions are like the questions you asked in the previous section when you first arrived in the community:

- Who are the decision-makers in the community?
- Who are the people who will be impacted by the work you are doing?

- Who are the people who disagree or are not interested in the work that you are doing?
- What nonprofits and organizations are doing similar work?
- What businesses would support (or oppose) the work that you are doing?
- Who else in the community stands to benefit from the work that you are doing?
- Who in the community may be negatively impacted by the work that you are doing?
- What would happen if nothing changed, and the status quo was maintained?

Your conversations and community engagement activities must include diverse perspectives and you must build relationships across all these constituencies if you wish to improve your chances of accomplishing lasting goals. In the previous example, the purpose is not for you to ultimately agree with what the traditional healer is saying. We have met many faith leaders, nonprofit organizations, and traditional healers whose beliefs we did not share, or who were taking an approach to their work that we could not endorse. But we also know that those faith leaders, nonprofit organizations, and traditional healers are very influential in their communities. If we do not factor in and understand the perspectives they bring to the spaces where they live and work, then they could ultimately undermine everything we try to do. To know those individuals and have a relationship with them and invite them to have a seat at the table is not to necessarily endorse everything they believe, but to engage them in the conversation equally.

Over the years, through the community development work we have done, we have had plenty of dinners with people with whom we disagree, and in some cases do not particularly like that much. But when you stand there and get to know them and truly listen to their perspective, two things happen. First, you might change your mind about some issues on which you did not think you had any room to move. And second, you will most definitely gather information about how their perspectives influence others, which will be invaluable in your work. Subsequently, as you run across opposition among others in the community, you will at least have insight into its origins.

As we said before, if you take this approach, then you have to be open to changing the way you think about an issue; even if academia or society deem you the "expert."

"Adapting on the Fly: Developing a Community of Scholars from Afar,"
by: Thomas Karrel

The year 2020 was strange and challenging for all of us. The COVID-19 pandemic drastically changed the way our global community interacts, moves, and receives education and learning opportunities. At GLI, the primary scope of my work is focused on what we call the "Global Classroom." These are programs involving cross-cultural exchange and collaboration among various students, scholars and other community leaders interested in learning about, researching, and doing good community development work. Typically, our global classroom operates primarily through travel, and immersing people from the United States in conversations and experiences with individuals from Uganda and Rwanda. The news in early 2020 about a novel coronavirus potentially changing the fabric of our society was a crushing blow, and meant we had to immediately reframe and rethink our approach. Our core services that we provided through the GLI were about to fundamentally change and we had very little time to listen, think, and act.

The idea to take our experiential courses, immersion trips, and student internships to a virtual space had been discussed prior to COVID-19. The pandemic, however, kicked this to the top of our priority list. Like many other organizations around the world, we tried to create an innovative learning space in a virtual setting. And to our surprise, it worked better than we had ever imagined!

In 2020, we designed a virtual fellowship program that would offer university students and young professionals an opportunity to connect with dozens of unique community development leaders from various countries in East Africa and the US. Fellows would be part of daily conversations surrounding foreign aid, neo-colonialism, education, public health, research, environment, economic development, and many other areas. This was listening. We challenged each of our fellows to seek to understand perspectives and build empathy with leaders from around the world and ask specific questions and share about their own experiences.

Additionally, each participant would be part of a collaborative research group to tackle real-world development questions posed by GLI's community partners in East Africa. This was thinking and acting. Fellows met each week to collect data about a thematic area of development, guided by a GLI team member who facilitated regular dialogues with the group members to form strong working relationships. One group, consulting for a Ugandan social enterprise on early childhood education issues, even went as far as fundraising $3,000 to support ongoing literacy projects, and created a long-term partnership with the organization's staff.

We were aiming to create legitimate spaces for the emerging leaders of our world to form genuine connections about community development work and build relationships. And these relationships did not just end in the confines of the Zoom calls but have led to numerous internships and research projects with GLI and several of our community partners.

During the next year, we convened four five-week cohorts of fellows to meet over Zoom to learn about all aspects of international and local community development, how to build relationships with one another, and engage in collaborative research projects. We had 86 university students and young professionals from around the globe including the United States, Uganda, Rwanda, and Kenya take part in this program. Because of our strong connection to the local communities through our Ugandan-based team, dozens of these scholars continue their research projects and maintain relationships with their peers and our organization and in-country partners.

We will be the first to tell you that you cannot fully recreate in-person educational experiences virtually. With COVID-19, we were limited to a two-dimensional world, full of connectivity issues, scheduling challenges, and plenty of awkward Zoom silences. For students and scholars who want to work in foreign countries, it is imperative to physically go there to engage properly. However, the virtual fellowship we built taught us that there is massive potential for a different approach to learning and cross-cultural collaboration—an approach that can include students who might never have the opportunity to travel to Africa otherwise.

The community of young people we recruited through our virtual fellowship program inspired us. Hundreds of young people across the United States and East Africa came to the table to listen, think, and act together with our partner organizations, and served as a reminder for us that at the heart of education and community development work is the importance of forging strong relationships no matter what the obstacles.

———

Whether it's a homeless veteran from urban Colorado or a woman from a rural village in southern Uganda, the people you seek to interact with will know when you are the real deal. They can tell the difference between being genuinely asked to be part of something and offered a seat at the table and when they are there just for the optics. If you are not behaving like the real deal when working with hard-to-reach populations, you may permanently damage any relationships you have built. When you are not authentic, you risk losing the trust of the community where you work and can seriously compromise your ability to impact change.

Do not invite someone to the table just because they represent a certain race, culture, or social group that you know you need to have represented. If you have no intention of truly hearing out someone's perspective, no matter how contrarian it might be, then do not invite them. There is no room for tokenism in true relationship building.

In reference back to the Denver case studies and the community work with the homeless, as these groups were building out programming, they listened to the city council and local business leaders; they listened to the district police at their weekly community meetings and the neighbors at their association meetings. They listened to donors and to other nonprofit homeless providers. But above all, they listened to the people whom they served. People experiencing homelessness had a real seat at the table, not a symbolic chair.

Including all your stakeholders in the design of programs is not just the right thing to do, it is the smart thing to do. Good community development teams understand the people they serve almost as well as the communities understand themselves. If you want to be an expert on homeless youth in urban America and design innovative, strategic, and high-impact programs, then you should ask the homeless youth what they think. You should build relationships with homeless youth. If you want to serve teachers around a lake in rural Uganda to design better early childhood education programs for the community, then you should ask the teachers what they think. You should build relationships with those teachers.

If you finish reading this chapter and take away one more lesson on good community development, be sure to listen to the people and build genuine relationships with all the key stakeholders. Genuine relationships are based on honesty and trust and take time to build. They begin with sharing stories, empathy for one another's lives, and an equitable idea exchange. Genuine relationships will not easily fizzle out, and they should be synergistic, producing an outcome that helps both parties reach their higher potential.

From private sector decision-making to nonprofit interventions, the litmus test is not whether you merely include the people you serve, but if you genuinely listen and think with them.

―――――

"The Skyline Park Parable: The Truth is On the Street," by: Jamie Van Leeuwen

I remember when the Downtown Denver Partnership decided to reinvent Skyline Park on the 16th Street Mall. For a street kid or a skater kid or any kid for that matter, Skyline Park was an urban paradise, with massive rock formations, fountains, and caves all engineered for fun in the middle of downtown on the main pedestrian thoroughfare.

> *Additional Learning: Constructed between 1972 and 1975, this one-acre linear park and plaza was a central feature of the Skyline Urban Renewal District, a revitalization plan conceived in the 1950s for Lower Downtown Denver. Designed by Lawrence Halprin, the plaza was intended as an urban oasis and gateway to central downtown. The three-block design was sunken below street level and heavily planted along the edges, with a continuous berm to separate the park and street, and concrete risers to access the space. Concrete was incorporated into retaining walls, stepped seating walls, planters, and abstract fountains. Reminiscent of natural rocky outcroppings, these rectilinear concrete forms reflected the nearby red stone foothills, while horizontal banding on the park's concrete walls evoked natural stone striations and provided a visual and spatial connection between site elements (The Cultural Landscape Foundation, 2020).*

It was curious to listen to how upset the downtown business executives and members of the area's burgeoning residential community got as the kids would hang out, make out, and smoke out all day in this Disney-like stage complete with hiding spaces, skateboard ramps, and great places to sit. The powers-that-be had built something that screamed to a teenager to come and chill, especially if one was homeless and had nothing else to do. The simple message here is if you do not want homeless teenagers to hang out in your park, then do not make it look ridiculously fun and awesome!

And I remember when the city leaders began the process to redesign it. The park advisory committee hosted focus groups of business leaders, non-profit workers, and police officers to get a sense of how they could recreate the park to engage more than just street kids. While they included the kids in the redesign of the new park, complete with skateboard ramps and places to sit, they did not inquire about location; the park was constructed outside of the central downtown area. Millions of dollars could have been saved and better outcomes achieved with a simple question to the target population: "if we build this other park in a new location, will you leave the downtown area?" This was the right question.

They successfully re-engineered historic Skyline Park, removing all the cavernous landscaping that made it unique. And to lure the kids away from the downtown pedestrian traffic, they built a beautiful state-of-the-art skate park several blocks off the pedestrian mall. Had the park advisory committee actually listened to the kids, what they would have learned was that the primary reason that homeless kids went to Skyline Park was not just because it was fun; it was because it was on the Mall and it was a great place for them to interact with other people! They felt safe at the park, and they could access services and spare change at the heart of the city. They wanted to be where the rest of the city's people were. When the city leaders rebuilt the park with the idea that the kids would go to another more engaging location, some of the kids kept stubbornly returning to the more boring version of the old park and continued to hang out, make out, and smoke out.

Relationships were the missing ingredient here. The park advisory committee did not establish any relationships with the young people in the area, and viewed this project as a partnership with the local community. The committee should have sent representatives out to spend time with the young people hanging out at Skyline Park. Find out what the experience was like for the young people frequenting the park each day, having conversations, and establishing a genuine collaboration.

The City acted without listening or thinking. Before they did something, they should have stood there, exchanged ideas with the youth population, and built a legitimate partnership to reach a common goal for urban Denver.

———

In this case we see a specific example on how exchanging ideas and building relationships could have led the design team to ask the right questions.

You can be the best listener on the planet but if you do not ask the right question(s), you will be disappointed in your outcomes. Therein lies the lesson of this section. We do not always listen, and we do not always offer a seat at the table to the people who can best help us solve complex (or even simple) social problems. We are especially prone to forget to include the very people we hope to serve. Even when all of this happens, timing matters. In this case, the design team listened to the kids and created a seat at the table after they came up with the idea that they wanted to implement. What would this project have looked like if they had started with input from the youth about the idea itself?

Give your constituents a meaningful voice in the dialogue at the very beginning and build meaningful relationships. While it can upset the rest of the table at times, your community work will render more enduring forms of success.

Engineering Consensus: The Art of Finding Common Ground

Now that you have stood there and built relationships and listened to the people that you are serving, what are your intentions? Especially when you are working on something where not everyone is in consensus, finding common ground is challenging. This has grown even more common as social media and contrasting narratives tug at all of us. Increasingly our world draws information from myriad different outlets, many of them online and ill-sourced. Finding common ground is an art in politics, community development, and business. Common ground is the base you need to create for good community development work to last, whether you are solving homelessness in the western United States or building out an agricultural cooperative in Northern Uganda.

What you need to understand about common ground is that we do not have to agree on everything to do community development work and improve livelihoods. What specific things can we find to agree upon? Consensus can come in all different shapes and sizes. Put a group of five people in a room from different geographic sectors, socioeconomic backgrounds, and ethnicities and you could spend the remainder of your life trying to resolve all the differences on matters where this group disagrees. But without too much effort you could probably find one or two things about which they agree. That is consensus.

Take a charged issue like immigration in the United States. Immigration policy is rooted in polarizing politics with diverse opinions on issues like the DREAM Act (Development, Relief, and Education for Alien Minors), DACA (Deferred Action for Childhood Arrivals), border crossings, access to public benefits, and the building of a border wall. President Trump made it one of his key election issues for 2016 and there is a case to be made that it was one of the stances that led him to victory. Yet a Gallup Poll reported on July 1, 2020, that "nearly eight in ten (77%) of Americans think immigration is a good thing for their country" (Younis, 2020). Amid the many things that we disagree on about immigration, we mostly agree that it is a good thing for the country. So why not start there?

With an issue as polarizing as immigration, start in a place as fundamental as general agreement that immigration is good for the country, to build the work around that point at which you can find consensus. If you start with whether a group of people thinks America should build a wall to prevent undocumented people from entering the country, or whether the country should grant all undocumented people living in the United States full citizenship, then you have started with the extremes, and you will almost certainly have a longer road to consensus. Instead, by starting with whether people believe that immigration is good for the country, you have begun your relationship building in a place of agreement and you can subsequently move together to the harder topics ahead.

Once you have built relationships and seated the table, you must then begin the hard work of ensuring authenticity. Common ground thrives on authenticity, and it is hard to find compromise or agreement if the people seated at the table doubt the sincerity of one another. What attracts everyone? What are their intentions? From there, work on how you will resolve differences, and in some cases endeavor to set those differences aside in the interest of moving forward toward a collective goal. Finding common ground takes practice and patience and artful negotiation back and forth. It is not for the faint of heart. Unfortunately, in the world of community development, we do not see this happen enough. We in the development world seem to either spend our time arguing about subjects on which we disagree and are unlikely to resolve, or we decide to go our separate ways, do our own thing, and forgo compromise and collaboration. At which point, there are a lot of different people rowing in a lot of different directions.

Few examples jump to mind that highlight this stronger than GLI's public health music festival battle in Lira, Uganda with a group of foreign volunteers.

———

"Aren't We On The Same Team?," by: Thomas Karrel

GLI and a network of local partners have been putting on music festivals across Uganda and Rwanda since 2014, with a focus on cultural exchange and public health. We will hear more about the concerts in Chapter Six, so let me jump into a specific instance in August 2018 when our team faced an unexpected adversary: another international development organization.

We held our first concert in Lira, Uganda, in 2016. The model for our concerts was developed over years, born out of a collective interest to bring Uganda and American musicians together for live art and cultural exchange, coupled with local health providers' desire to reach larger audiences with HIV testing and other health services. The model was locally driven, and over the years has brought hundreds of thousands of people together to get important health services and information, and to have fun.

We connected with volunteers from another international organization working in Lira, who immediately found the concert model exciting and saw its potential. However, the workers from this organization were all foreign, and would be leaving the following year. The next group of volunteers that participated wanted nothing to do with GLI and our concert series.

Our team was planning our biggest concert to-date in Lira in late 2018 and began engaging in conversations with this organization early on. We wanted to know who the volunteers were partnering with, how we could exchange ideas, and ultimately elevate both of our development agendas. But we were met with consistent animosity and disinterest in any partnership.

Fast forward to July 2018, a month before our concert in Lira. We find out that both GLI and this other organization had gained approval from the Lira local government to have health-related events on the same day, at the same venue in downtown Lira. Great news! We were psyched. This was the perfect opportunity to collaborate, as their event was also related to health service delivery. Our concert was bringing in the top performing artists from around Uganda, with local dance troupes from Lira and several American musicians. This would be our biggest and best concert yet and a great opportunity for us to model collaboration.

However, weeks before the concert, we found out that the volunteers running the other event not only did not want to collaborate with us but were in fact upset as they believed they were "there first", and that our concert was overshadowing their event. They waved their local government approval letter in front of us as if it was a deed to the Lira community.

This was crazy. We were expecting upwards of 20,000 people at our concert and had been working with local health partners and community groups for several years to produce these shows. The only agreement we could reach was that their event would take place during the day, on the other side of the venue, and they would stop promptly at sundown so we could commence our concert program. Such a missed opportunity, but we were open to the compromise.

Instead, the group set up their event tents in the middle of our concert grounds and refused to take them down at dusk as agreed. They were actively sabotaging the agreement we had reached. We did not understand. Shouldn't we all be on the same team when it comes to community development work?

Their negative actions only continued when they refused to share their health data with our team, as we had previously agreed. While our team shared all our primary data from the concerts with their group, they used our information in their report, taking credit for the impact of our concert.

This is not a story intended to criticize; but rather to highlight a crucial point on building relationships. The actions of this group of foreign volunteers were a net negative on both our organizations, not to mention the local community and government, who later expressed anger and resentment at the damaged relationships caused by the active dismissal of logical and simple collaboration.

These were foreign volunteers who did not speak the local language, and were making critical decisions for the Lira community about how health services and information should be disseminated. Unfortunately, this story is not unique and is one of so many missed opportunities for genuine collaboration and coalition building in international community development; not to mention wasted resources.

This encounter highlights an unfortunate reality I have come to understand: in community development, oftentimes the primary obstacle to an initiative comes from other development workers, through turf issues and ego investment that compromises the ability to deliver much-needed services and support to under-resourced communities. At times, development workers can be more invested in projecting and sharing about the work they are doing, rather than focusing on the work itself.

There are so many instances in community development work where clear opportunities for collaboration and relationship building between international organizations are sacrificed. As Merton reminds us, the truth is in the work.

———

This story should further bolster the idea that relationship building in community development is not easy. It takes time, and mutual respect and understanding between organizations, local governments, and community members. As you take on this aspect of relationship building, which is only effective when listening and thinking have been embraced, here are some more questions to consider:

- What are the deal breakers in the room?
    - What are the issues that, if we put them on the table too early, will cause us to lose stakeholders?
- When considering all of the stakeholders involved, what are their intentions?
    - What are they hoping to achieve by being part of this conversation?
    - What are the shared intentions where our concerns overlap?
- If we cannot get consensus, can we get to a place where folks agree but with reservations?
    - Can we achieve enough compromise that we can move the plan forward, even if we do not all love every piece of it?
    - Can we all endorse a plan that articulates common ground, even as we acknowledge there may still be some things we wish were different?

Let us go back again to the homeless commission described in Chapter One and think about how the members responded to these questions as a diverse group of community leaders who worked together to find common ground to advance a major homelessness initiative in Denver. The emphasis here being that good community development means making sure everyone has a seat at the table and fostering an understanding that when people exercise their authentic voices, not everyone will cordially agree. Yet taking the time to understand the intentions of everyone is critical.

As the homeless commission evolved, representatives from the business community pushed back on the notion that they were greedy, uncaring merchants who wanted the unhoused to go away. They were not the "haters" they were made out to be. Instead, they were business owners whose businesses were being impacted by people sleeping in front of their doorsteps and urinating in their back alleys.

The homeless providers pushed back on the notion that they were liberal "do-gooders" who wanted the homeless to be able to do whatever they pleased at the expense of the taxpayer. Instead, they were human rights advocates who cared deeply about making sure everyone had a decent place to sleep and an alternative to living on the streets. And they believed in accountability.

Through the process of developing a better understanding of the intentions of all the people involved, relationships improved, stereotypes dissipated, and the stakeholders could then turn their attention to finding a way forward together. Truly taking the time to listen, think, and understand the real intentions of the other people and being willing to adjust perspectives and change opinions is a model for how to effect change that we need now more than ever. This is a lesson that we need to embrace locally, nationally, and internationally, as dialogue in the political world has grown increasingly vitriolic and divisive.

As stated throughout this chapter, when working on issues ranging from homelessness to human trafficking, it is quite easy to find issues and approaches on which we disagree. The art is to take the lessons derived from the kinds of experiences described here and apply them to finding the common ground that anchors stakeholders and allows community development work to move forward collectively, through honest and enduring relationships.

Caveat emptor, let the buyer beware. The road to common ground and relationship building is not as smooth as this text may make it out to be. It is always hard to apply book-learning to real-life situations. We can offer examples from our lives to inform you and give you different perspectives, but every situation you encounter will be unique and have nuances that you might not have anticipated or seen covered in any book. The objective we hope you leave with is to adapt the lessons you learn in this text to best fit the work you are doing in the communities where you serve.

What do you do if you cannot find common ground? What if there is a stakeholder who is never going to get on board?

At some point, after you have done your due diligence, there is a time when you may have to move on. You have built strong relationships and you have stood there, and you have listened. You have authentically created a seat at the table and made sure that all voices and perspectives are represented, even those with whom you disagree. You have done the thinking, and you have spent time finding common ground. If at the end of the day, among your collective stakeholders there are persons who just cannot find consensus with the rest of the group, it is reasonable to part ways. If you have included everyone in the process and made genuine effort to ensure that all voices are heard, and your group reaches an inflection point and needs to move forward, there are cases in community development where you must move forward with noted objections.

Summing Up

Everything in this chapter is intended to get you to think intentionally about how the work that you hope to do depends upon the quality of the relationships you build. Relationships are the bedrock that support the design process of community development. We have a good friend and colleague who makes this point well:

"Relationship building is absolutely critical to the success of any organization. To do that effectively, you first have to dedicate time to listening to the people who you are trying to form relationships with. You have to understand their background, interests, needs, and motivation."
- *Phil Dimon, Foreign Service Officer (Public Affairs), United States State Department*

Many leaders and community organizations like to say that they collaborate, but few actually do. This is an important note to end on as sometimes in community development, collaboration is equated with dividing labor or sharing tasks. While such activities are helpful and can foster common ground and build relationships, they are not the same as developing legitimate collaboration. Take the Skyline Park example, where the design team truly believed they were collaborating with the youth, when in fact they were simply consulting them. There was no true role for the local youth to play in the decision-making process and the power was all in the hands of the design team. It is not that different from a symbolic chair where being at the table does not mean you are legitimately heard, valued, or given power. Each of these illusions can be distinguished from true collaboration by both the nature of the relationship and outcomes of the interaction.

Community development is messy, and it does not always work the way we want it to. Building relationships likely will not turn out exactly the way that we have outlined. Instead, as students and practitioners of good community development, use the core tenets of standing there, creating seats at the table, and finding common ground in a less linear approach. This book provides you with some of the core ingredients of good community development, but how you mix them all together will depend on the recipe and the community that you are serving.

The more you do this work, the better you will get at adjusting as you go along. Listen. Think. Act. is an iterative approach and has to be done over and over again to improve outcomes. If you put your trust in the work, the results will come. Building relationships and creating consensus can be unpredictable and hard, but you will get better at it as you gain practice. This will in turn build out your résumé of failures which we will discuss next in Chapter Five. Good community development looks different with each community and with each issue being addressed. Nobody can anticipate what will take place in novel circumstances, and often the best practitioners are simply those who are the most willing to learn from their inevitable mistakes.

CHAPTER FOUR "COMMUNITY CHANGEMAKER" CHALLENGE: IDEATE

Okay, now you have dived headfirst into your topic, and have defined the specific challenge you are aiming to solve. Time to get creative!

1. Your task now is to think: "How might we solve ___ problem with our user?"
   - Brainstorm and sketch out at least five different ideas! Be creative, and do not define your approach under terms that are overly strict. How would you solve this problem if you have $0? How about $1 billion? The innovators at Stanford, IDEO, Stanford, and Tulane's Taylor Center have shown us that it's extra helpful to use visuals in this step. Test out your drawing skills, Picasso! Visualize your ideas.
2. As you are brainstorming solutions to your problem, also take some time to walk through the phases of relationship building, setting the table, and finding common ground. As it relates to your issues at hand, think about these questions:
   - Who are the people who need to be seated at the table as we brainstorm ideas?
   - What are their intentions in participating?

- Is anyone missing from the brainstorming process and if so, who?
- Where do you think the various stakeholders may have common ground?
- What do you think it will take to move things forward?

In this phase we really want you to be creative! Channel your inner child a bit and do not be afraid to generate off-the-wall ideas. Even if they do not seem practical at first, they may help yield more easy-to-implement ideas or provide pieces of information you can use later. There are no wrong answers here!

CHAPTER FOUR CONVERSATION STARTERS

- In your opinion, what characteristics define a strong relationship or partnership?
- What is one professional relationship in your life that has served you well?
- How have your relationships enhanced or amplified the reach of your work?
- What does finding common ground look like in your community?
- What organizations or institutions are in place that can help you reach consensus in community development?
- Does your local government build consensus well?
- In the case where you cannot achieve common ground, how would you proceed?
- In a world where social media can drive misperceptions and create division, what do you think we need to do to help foster common ground?
- Can you think of a community development initiative locally or domestically that did not work out the way it was intended?
  - What happened?
  - Are there questions from this chapter that the stakeholders should have addressed but did not?
  - As an emerging community development expert, what would you do differently?

- Goodwin, D. K. (2005). *Team of Rivals: The Political Genius of Abraham Lincoln.* Simon & Schuster.
- Goodwin, D. K. (2019). *Leadership: In Turbulent Times.* Simon & Schuster.
- Martin, C. (2016, April 23). *Western do-gooders need to resist the allure of "exotic problems."* The Guardian.
- McChrystal, G. S., Collins, T., Silverman, D., & Fussell, C. (2015). *Team of Teams: New Rules of Engagement for a Complex World* (Illustrated ed.). Portfolio.
- Merton, T. (1966, February 21). *Letter to a Young Activist.* Merton.org.
- Milliner, B. L. (2005). (rep.). *Denver's Ten-Year Plan to End Homelessness 2005-2015* (pp. 1-32). Denver, CO: Denver's Road Home.
- Novogratz, J. (2009). *The Blue Sweater: Bridging the Gap Between Rich and Poor in an Interconnected World* (1st ed.). Rodale Books.
- Williams, M. (2019, November 8). *Why I'll Never Go on a Mission Trip Again - ZORA.* Medium.

PART III: ACT

In Part III: ACT, we move into the final phase of our Listen. Think. Act. community development process. This section explores the stage when organizations and individuals make use of their many ideas, research, and insights in the form of real-world initiatives and programs that aim to address complex societal issues. First, we review your résumé of failures, as community development practitioners need to understand that failures are inevitable, and experimentation is how innovation and progress happen. Next is the whole shebang: creating lasting impact. What does this look like in practice? What we can say for certain is this: at the heart of long-term impact is local ownership and legitimately sustainable ideas. But we need to explore the meaning of these terms further.

"Be open-minded, and don't be defined by the confines that society wants you to adhere to… I'm hoping to take my experience abroad and [use] everything I've learned and turn it into something that can benefit people in my own community."
– Jonathan Wells, Cornell University student; 2019 GLI International Youth
Summit Participant

CHAPTER FIVE
Innovate Through Experimentation:
Learning Through Failure and Change

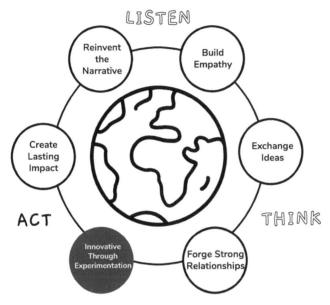

"I have come to learn to be patient and not to give up too quickly. It takes patience and persistence to bring a new and innovative product and ways of doing things to a community. There are early adopters who immediately embrace the product and there are traditionalists who resist the change that the initiative represents."
- Bernice Dapaah, co-founder of Ghana Bamboo Bikes Initiative in Ghana.

"In my experience, in Africa there is space for innovation. And you don't have to look far, especially when you are at a disadvantage. Look around you. You might be experiencing a problem that is a need in the community."
- Sizwe Nzima, founder of Iyeza Express in Khayelitsha, South Africa.

We are now at a place where your community development toolbox is starting to fill up with skills, techniques, and best practices that can be taken with you wherever you do your work. You know the importance of listening and thinking before you act, and that story sharing, empathy building, exchanging ideas, and relationship building are all vital. Each stage matters for practitioners and defines how you engage in community development, driving the degree of impact and the quality of outcomes for the people being served. But to get better at what you do and to take on the complex social issues that we all confront in community development work every day, you need to factor in the critical role that experimentation and innovation play.

We included two quotes here as they are both relevant to our discussion ahead. Patience and persistence make a difference, and there is no question that African countries have space for innovation. How you harness patience and persistence and create a space for innovation will be measured by your résumé of failures. The most successful community development practitioners begin with a very long and established list of failures. Your level of success in innovation and experimentation will be driven by how you embrace the idea that failure is inevitable in community development work.

Do not worry, successes will come too! We hope this chapter does not dissuade you from ever taking action in communities. Action is what we are all working towards, and in Chapter Six we will take you through some of our own successes. In community development, failures are endemic, and recognition of preliminary failures in your work is not just likely, but inevitable. If approached right, however, this recognition will help you find the right path and will warrant a proper celebration once you reach truly successful outcomes in your work.

Community Development in Action

When you hear the word "development," what comes to mind? More money? Better health? Less violence? Happier people?

A student of international development might jump in and highlight public health and economic programs. They might use indicators—observable changes or markers for measuring various statistical points—to gauge work focused on malaria and HIV prevention or improved reproductive health services. A government official or economist might see development as increasing Gross Domestic Product (GDP) or median income to strengthen a community. Maybe your answer involves more about the environment and climate change; maybe your answer speaks of access to essential services like clean water, food, and shelter. Maybe it advocates for LGBTQ populations and the rights of women or persons with disabilities. Or maybe your mind goes to the strength of relationships in a community, and the collective state of mental health.

PeerNetBC defines community development as "a process where community members come together to take collective action and generate solutions to common problems" (PeerNetBC, 2020). More generally, the *Cambridge Dictionary* defines it as "the activity of working with people from a particular area in order to try to improve their quality of life" (Cambridge University Press, 2021). And we defined good community development in the Prologue of this book as an approach to social change which maximizes collective well-being of a target population and limits suffering from preventable problems.

Development can hold many different meanings. The process, as well as the outcomes, will vary depending on the context and audience in question. Regardless of your definition, it is important for practitioners around the world to understand what constitutes good community development work and success in their own context. Fundamental questions must be confronted by governments, nonprofits, scholars, philanthropists, business leaders, activists, and citizens. How can nations foster healthy societies that promote well-being? How can aid or development programs be made effective and sustainable? What examples of good development exist in the world today and how can others model that process?

From the nonprofit and philanthropic perspective, organizations usually draw on a limited pool of resources from private foundations, corporations, governments, and individual donors. But the field is changing and innovations like social impact investing and universal income strategies are reinventing public-private-nonprofit partnerships to leverage scarce resources more effectively.

Do the efforts of the nonprofit sector aimed at securing these resources increase the capacity to effect change in fields such as health, education, and public management? Or do these interventions diminish overall local development capacity? And with social impact investing rapidly becoming popular, what is the role of the private sector in alleviating poverty around the world? Do corporations have an obligation to get involved? How we answer these questions in practice speaks directly to how organizations and individuals are challenged with improving the lives of people in all sorts of communities around the world.

To address these questions, we need to learn from the listening and thinking and acting we have already done and build on both our successes and failures. We will learn what works as we reflect upon our résumé of successes, but we will also learn what doesn't work and will likely amass an even more extensive résumé of failures. This is true in all aspects of social and scientific work. You do not usually find the cure or the solution on the first try. As of April 4,

2021, there were more than 50 clinical trials taking place around the world to identify viable vaccines for COVID-19, and at the time only four had been approved (Grün, 2021). How many versions of the vaccine have been tried that did not work? How many times did we fail before we got half a dozen vaccines that succeeded?

Failures are where a large portion of community development learning takes place.

Résumé of Failures

By this point, we hope we have inculcated the importance of listening, thinking, and acting in guiding your community development work. We have repeatedly urged you to refrain from just doing something and have encouraged you to stand there. We have emphasized the importance of empathy and relationship-building and exchanging ideas with one another. With all that said, good community development and transformation ultimately requires action. And at some point, as a practitioner of community development you cannot just stand there any longer.

Here is where it gets complicated, and we are going to attempt to thread the needle. While we think there is great risk in acting without thinking, we also worry that conversely it is possible for people to succumb to listening and thinking and listening and thinking repeatedly without ever taking a risk and acting on what they have learned. Again, we believe in an iterative process, and action is only warranted after you have taken the first two steps: listen and think. Organizations, especially public sector institutions, can get so caught up in their strategic planning, needs assessments, and research that by the time they finish planning, the context of the community has changed, and they need to start all over again. Listen and think... but then, if you have achieved consensus, act! When you have the data and you have successfully engaged the local community in genuine interchange, empower the team you have assembled to take what you have learned together and let them run with it. Pay attention to what you still need to learn and adjust as you go along. We will talk about measuring impact and how data informs your work later in the chapter, but for the time being, we want to focus on getting you out of the starting gate.

As practitioners, we argue that your "résumé of failures" should be many pages longer than your résumé of accomplishments. If you do not have 20 things you have tried that have not worked, then you should probably think bigger! In community development work, we are addressing big problems that will require a lot of work to figure out. We are only going to succeed after we see what went wrong on our first, second, and third tries

Even when you spend time listening and thinking, you may still fail when you act, at least in some respects. Yet if you learn along the way and you do not make the same mistake again, then you are practicing good community development. Lee Iacocca, an iconic CEO who orchestrated the turn-around of Chrysler in the 1980s, had a great insight into business that also applies to community development work: "mistakes are a part of life; you can't avoid them. All you can hope is that they won't be too expensive and that you don't make the same mistake twice" (Iacocca, 2011).

Looking back on the evolution of the GLI, the team's résumé of failures started with the idea that we would bring new interactive SMART boards to every classroom in Uganda and Rwanda. But for the most part, the technology never got used because rural schools lacked electricity. Then, we tried candle making with a local Women's Association, and later we tried launching a boat taxi service to improve transportation networks and access to the markets but failed again in both instances. We will tell you about our eventual successes, but first let us look at what we did wrong. True to Iacocca, one might say mistakes have been a part of life at GLI, and we have been lucky they have not been too expensive. We have also worked hard not to make the same mistake twice.

———

"A Candle Making Conundrum on Lake Bunyonyi," by Jamie Van Leeuwen

Our organization spent extensive time listening to a local association formed by women from villages around Lake Bunyonyi. These women clearly wanted to acquire practical skills that would help them generate more income. They said they wanted to learn paper making, candle making, and beekeeping. All seemed like potential revenue generators at the local markets, not to mention the burgeoning tourist industry around the lake. Candle making seemed like a smart place to start. Who doesn't need a candle? The local communities needed candles. The hotels needed candles. What tourist wouldn't love to leave the lake with a candle they bought from a local women's association? Candles that support community development from their proceeds. Hell, we could even start exporting them to the United States and have students sell them around the country!

Listen and think. We learned about the candle making process and what it would take for Entusi Resort and Retreat Center and GLI to take it on. The women were enthusiastic, and our local staff embraced the idea. We priced out candle-making machines and found we could buy a used one for a good price. We talked to the local hotel managers around Lake Bunyonyi and several of them said they would be interested in buying our candles. We talked to some of our guests, and they liked the idea. One of our student interns even figured out how to package the candles in really great boxes; the design was fantastic. And we did it right. We did not decide one day to make candles, but rather did a lot of listening and a lot of thinking before we acted.

A community leader in Denver who was committed to women's empowerment loved the idea and helped us purchase the candle making machine. We put together a plan and started production. We were going to sustain the work we did at the GLI and at the Entusi community center on Lake Bunyonyi through candles alone. We would be candle tycoons in no time and the *Chronicle of Philanthropy* would feature us on the front page of their journal!

Our first batch was awesome! They looked great and we were ready for distribution. But there was a problem. As we started to market the candles, we quickly learned that the diameter of the candles we were making did not fit any of the standard holders that you would place a candle in around the lake. The dimensions were off, and the locals did not like them. Argh!

So, we changed the size, produced another batch, and there was an interest in buying our candles locally, but not for the price that we were charging. Our costs of production were too high, and the candle markets were far more competitive than we had understood. We had taken on the Indian grocers who could buy candles in bulk and sell them at low prices, and our ability to compete with them in the local community was just never going to happen.

Our foreign guests would pay for candles of such quality, but again the dimensions we were producing were not consistent with United States candle holders; they just did not fit. Folks would buy them but there was no easy way to use them. And you had to sell a hell of a lot of candles to make the math work. We tried a few more iterations and we came to a decision-making point about how to proceed. We listened and thought and acted. And as we acted, we listened and thought some more, and then we thought again. Finally, we reached that moment where we had to decide where this project fit in the overall work. On our résumé of successes? Or on our résumé of failures?

We were at that point that Iacocca warned of: we knew our mistakes were at risk of becoming expensive and we did not want to keep making the same mistakes over and over. And with that we were out of the candle-making business.

P.S. We do have a candle-making machine for sale if anyone is interested!

———

Sometimes a project that you add to your résumé of failures can still lead to a success… unintentionally. As a practitioner, over time you will get better at trusting your gut. Your experience and your instincts will guide you and you will eventually make more informed decisions. In turn, you will (or should) also take bigger risks. That is how innovation happens. And no matter how in tune you are with your work, the way events turn out will still surprise you along the way.

Take the Lake Bunyonyi boat taxi service as another example and entry on GLI's résumé of failures… and successes.

———

"Monopoly Busting Boats on Lake Bunyonyi," by Jamie Van Leeuwen

Lake Bunyonyi is 25 kilometers long, seven kilometers wide and has at least 29 islands. Basically, Lake Bunyonyi is a big lake, and there are two ways to get to the markets: by walking or by boat (Gningui, 2020). Unless you have a seaplane! Boat travel is relatively expensive for locals and if you are trying to get your goods to the markets and happen to live on the other end of the lake, you need to decide if the cost to take a boat there and back will be more or less than what you will earn by selling your goods. And people around the lake do not just need boats for the markets. If their mom gets sick or their wife is pregnant, people need boats to get to the doctor. In situations when you must charter a boat and you live in a rural village on the lake, it is not all that different from having to buy a plane ticket to get you from Denver to Colorado Springs in a pinch. Point being, it is not cheap.

Having learned from our candle making debacle, we did our homework. We gathered the data we would need to inform our decision on how to make transportation around the lake more accessible and affordable. We had learned about barriers to transportation through a community-based needs assessment we had conducted with local families living on the shores of Lake Bunyonyi. We came up with the innovative idea of launching a boat taxi service that would stop at regular locations throughout the day and provide people with affordable boat services. We would subsidize the boat, generate revenue from the service, employ local workers, and, in turn, address one of the key needs of the community.

A group of business students at the University of Denver did a cost-benefit analysis. We figured out which stops would be the most popular and convenient, what would be the most fuel-efficient route, what was a fair price to charge, and how we could set up our business model to at least break even. We crunched the numbers; we bought a brilliant new boat that was financed by a generous donor, and we had a grand celebration to launch our new Entusi Boat Taxi Service. We were bringing more affordable transportation to the local community. Look out southern Uganda! Entusi and GLI are coming.

Skip ahead a couple of weeks into our new enterprise. I hopped a ride on the prized new taxi boat to go for a run into town one day, and as I got off at the dock, a group of local boat drivers sneered and hissed at me. They were upset, and before I could begin my errands, they aired their grievances. We at GLI had done a good job of listening and thinking with passengers who lived around the lake, but we had never spent time listening and thinking with these folks: the existing boat drivers. Their boats provided income for their families, and they relied on providing transportation to the locals to support their children. Along comes this well-funded Entusi boat, and now the local boat drivers couldn't compete. Prices went down, and their ability to operate grew untenable. Good community development is about connecting local communities with access to transportation, but it is not about driving 20 local entrepreneurs out of business because your boat is better than theirs. Like the parable of Skyline Park in Chapter Four, we did not listen from the street level (or the lake, in this case) on up.

We had a long conversation with the local boat drivers, and over the next couple of days we agreed that if we took our boat out of service as a taxi, they would reduce the high prices they had previously set and not take advantage of people by charging them unfair rates. We renegotiated the way our boat could be used, and it now serves as a primary source of transportation to get youth to their respective schools, so they do not have to spend two hours canoeing back and forth (BBC, 2017). Through listening and thinking and acting, we failed at first, but then we listened and thought again, and we ended up succeeding in a way we had never anticipated.

We love this story as it shows you the turns that community development can take when you are open to learning and shifting as you go along. It is not that different from cooking. The first time you make a complicated dish, it is probably not as good as the second or third time around. As you try the recipe each time, you learn how to make the food taste better; you learn how to get the flavor just right; and you learn to cook it for longer or on a higher heat. You adjust your cooking as you learn and then you try making the dish again. Community development is adjusting as you learn, and with each try, you should keep getting better. And with each success, you should try things that you haven't tried before. The more you fail, the longer your résumé of failures grows. However, you simultaneously get better at your work. And as your work improves, your résumé of successes also grows, and there are more beneficial impacts for the communities that you serve.

Before we leave this section, we want to end on a note of caution. Despite the inevitability of failure in practice, beware of it nonetheless as all community development workers need to be protective of the people and communities engaged. Development failures have consequences and are usually more serious for the community members than organizations. As discussed in Chapter Four, and the section on neo-colonialism, there is an indulgent kind of glorification of failure in some spheres in the United States. That is not the intent of this section. Embracing failure is not the same as going into your community development work with a reckless, macho attitude. Embracing failure is about considering the people and communities where you work and then acting bolding. While there is not a right way to fail, there is certainly a wrong way.

Defining Your Role in Action

As you experiment in your community development work and build out your résumé of failures, understanding your role will be important. Role confusion leads to inefficiencies and diminished returns and can ultimately lead to unintended or undesirable outcomes. Understanding funding sources and measuring impact is critical to conducting good community development. There are texts that can help hone these skills, and we want the reader to be aware of these models, how to navigate them, and how to factor them into real-world community work.

Current international development funding models are focused on three main functions: providing, managing, and spending. "Providing" is focused on amassing global funds which come from donor country governments, private foundations, businesses, and the public. "Managing" is concerned with the pooling and channeling of these funds to recipients. Examples of managing entities include the World Health Organization (WHO), United States Agency for International Development (USAID), Bill & Melinda Gates Foundation, World Bank, the European Commission, and thousands of international and local NGOs. The third function, "spending," is concerned with expenditure and consumption of these funds (Gumbie & Van Leeuwen, 2021).

While this landscape appears from the outside to be ordered, efficient, and simple, the reality on the ground is often a different story. NGOs for example, perform both managing and spending roles, while organizations like WHO and USAID are often involved in implementation as well as managing, thereby blurring the roles. When managing global health funds, these spending organizations often set the agenda by providing funding priorities and objectives. In turn, the spending organizations will then organize their projects according to those funding trends. Consequently, in many cases, funding priorities drive the spending, and run the risk of being misaligned with the actual needs of the communities being served. International development is complicated and the platform that is currently in place requires careful consideration. When funders and NGOs have not thoughtfully defined their roles, the funding can drive the work when ideally the needs of the community should drive the funding (Gumbie & Van Leeuwen, 2021).

The important takeaway here for the reader is to understand your role in this global network of development stakeholders. How funding is designated impacts local work and can propagate some of the neo-colonial approaches to community development that we discussed in earlier chapters. Good community development happens when the communities inform the funding, and the funder follows suit. Trouble comes when the funder assumes they know best what the community needs funding for (e.g. a school, a well, laptops) and grants their funds according to those assumptions.

Defining the Funding Relationship: Global Health

Global health funding appears to adhere to a needs-based approach following disease trends and emerging threats. For example, between 1990-1998, the plurality of global health funding went to health policy and management (29%), with 12% going to sexually transmitted infection (STI) control, including HIV. Between 1999-2004, a rapid shift in priorities saw a quarter of all global health funding (25%) directed towards STI control, including HIV

(OECD, 2006). This shift in global funding towards HIV and other STIs was not coordinated on a global level, leaving the door open for individual entities to determine funding priorities. Decisions were, in many cases, ineffective and sometimes counterproductive for the communities that were targeted; it was a missed opportunity for the global community to align its work more efficiently across funding platforms. For instance, 85% of donors reported allocating their funds on a 'needs' basis; however, the primary measure of 'needs' tended to be internally determined 'funding appeals.' These appeals are influenced by media conceptions and the popularity of global priorities, for example, climate change or infectious diseases. If we look at humanitarian assistance, we find that crisis response priorities are mostly led by needs assessments determined by outside entities. More than half (55%) of donor agencies use UN appeals as a measure of need. When 'need' remains ambiguous or too broadly defined, it is unlikely that funds are efficiently and effectively reaching the communities and projects where they can have the biggest impact (Dalrymple & Smith, 2015).

The system, as currently structured, is certainly capable of identifying some urgent needs, but has unintentionally created an international development approach that is, in many cases, driven more by nonprofit bureaucracies, media trends, appeals apparatus, and far-off assumptions than by community-based data and boots-on-the-ground intelligence. Strengthening the relationships with the people served by international community development initiatives is critical to creating the right structure that ultimately connects funding priorities to the actual needs of the intended communities. Good community development work means informing systems so that spending can better align with the direct needs of community members. In the same way that communications technology has learned to integrate across platforms, philanthropy and international community development need to demand this level of information-sharing and coordination to inform their decision-making. If we can instantaneously send a text to a friend on the other side of the planet thanks to having integrated telecommunications and computing into one mobile device, we can certainly work together to establish better, more efficient ways to make sure that someone living in a rural village who needs treatment can access care from practitioners who have factored in the context and the specific needs of the community in which they live.

Greater accountability for how programs are implemented needs to start with how the relationship between donor and recipient is defined. There can be dire consequences for a community when funding fails to hit its mark. Better donor-recipient alignment could prevent some of these failures and ultimately inform better outcomes, foster innovation, and promote accountability.

World-renowned educator and author Stephen Covey's principle rings very true here:

> "If the ladder is not leaning against the right wall, every step we take just gets us to the wrong place faster" (Covey, 2021).

The key takeaway here is to understand the role between the funder and the organization and ensure that the local community members drive the funding, not the outside funding organization. In communities where there are very limited resources, we see many instances where a funder ties their grant to a specific need, and the community acquiesces. Not because this is their top priority, but because they do not want to lose the funds or offend the influential donor. For example, take the funder who offers to build a school in a rural community where one does not exist. The community enthusiastically accepts the offer as they are getting something they did not have; however, had the founder asked the community what they really needed to meet their current development needs, building a school might not be among their top priorities.

Better community development will take place when communities can share their insights to better inform funders of their needs, and funding is designated accordingly. This is not to say that there should not be accountability and clearly established goals and outcomes to guide this work. These goals should be mutually agreed upon and an ongoing dialogue between development organizations, community members, and funders should take place to address obstacles that are encountered along the way. Funders and communities not adhering to this collaborative process—funding and local priorities are misaligned—leads to devastating outcomes from uninformed community development. This happens when we act before we listen and think. We see these detrimental effects in that beautiful school that is built which remains empty because there was no funding for the teachers, or the shallow well that worked until one of the parts broke and there was no way to repair or replace it locally.

There are so many ethical, political, financial, and strategic challenges that can be entangled in the context we are describing here. Our intention is to make the reader aware of these misguided practices as they grow in their role as a community development leader. Understanding and guiding the financial decisions of a community development organization is a critical skill. More importantly, teaching and empowering the communities to understand this approach to funding goes a long way to ensuring long-term sustainability.

Measuring and Evaluating Impact: Results Still Matter!

The issue of accountability leads us to the last key question in this chapter: how do we measure and evaluate impact as we innovate through experimentation? Experimentation can be transformative if you measure and assess your impact along the way. Otherwise, you have no idea if what you are doing is working and whether the effort will go on your résumé of failures or successes. Too often, there is a tendency in community development to introduce a new idea or concept, and then step back during implementation, when in fact we should be monitoring and assessing at every point along the way. Merton reminds us in his letter not to "depend on the hope of results" but rather "the truth of the work itself." While we agree that we do not want to measure our successes based solely on outcomes, data still matter, and they should factor into our experimentation.

When we talk about data, we do not only mean numbers. There is a range of information that can constitute as data, basically any relevant information, primary or secondary, that can help development actors better understand impacts and outcomes of their programs. Data should be gathered while listening and should directly inform the thinking and acting. Data also help uncover preconceived notions and biases.

Good community development is about building solid collaborations with partners in communities that can inform and contribute to positive outcomes. To generate good data, it is critical to conduct proper research, and helpful to have partners in place to support and inform that work. University and academic partnerships are some of the most underutilized alliances that nonprofit organizations can tap into in advising and driving their evaluation and assessments. These partnerships leverage resources and maximize impact. Nonprofits need rigorous evaluation and metrics to guide their listening, thinking, and acting in community development work. Conversely, academic institutions need on-the-ground projects and learning opportunities that can teach their students to be better researchers and practitioners. There is a symbiotic relationship here that has served GLI well over the years. Academic partners have helped inform both our organization and our local communities. Through dozens of different academic alliances, we have generated incredibly important data, evaluations, and needs assessments that we would not have been able to afford otherwise. And in turn, hundreds of undergraduate students, graduate students, and faculty have been offered a platform to hone their research skills and tackle real-world development questions that need to be answered. As we have listened to and thought about the extensive community-based research that has been generated through our academic partnerships, we have altered how we act, and ultimately improved both the quality of our work and outcomes for the communities with whom we collaborate.

———

"Slum Community Assumptions," by Jamie Van Leeuwen

Arguably one of the largest and most challenged neighborhoods in Uganda, the Katanga slum community stretches approximately 1.5 kilometers through central Kampala and is sandwiched between Uganda's national referral hospital, Mulago, and its largest and most prestigious public university, Makerere. Katanga is one of the first communities that GLI connected with in Uganda, and we have been working in partnership with organizations serving Katanga for over a decade. It is also where we conducted some of our preliminary research and needs assessments as we were in the early stages of learning to Listen. Think. Act. in Uganda.

In my first year of visiting Katanga, I thought it was very clear what the community members needed. In fact, given the abject poverty of the slum, the bigger question was, was there anything they did not need? Conditions in the slum are brutal, and I witnessed a level of raw poverty that I had not seen up close before. I made assumptions driven by my own biases; the experience of discovering that this truth resembled my encounter I had while working with Project Homeless Connect in Colorado, where the woman I was talking to wanted a playground for her kid. What I thought was important did not correlate perfectly to what the people of Katanga believed, and it surprised me when the results of our needs assessment came in. We learned and acted because of the data.

I assumed that a woman living in a tiny mud brick shanty located along the raw sewage ditch that ran through the center of Katanga would identify her primary needs for the six children living with her as better housing and sanitation. While she acknowledged both of those issues, when asked what she would prioritize spending money on if she had the choice, she said that what kept her up at night was the lack of access to education for her kids. Education. She had the foresight to know that while housing and sanitation were immediate needs, if she really wanted her family to thrive, they would require education to move out of the slum.

The data confirmed this to be the case in our surveys, and we published a study accordingly in partnership with the University of Colorado Denver and Creighton University (Van Leeuwen et al., 2017). The results of this study would serve to inform other nonprofits providing services in Katanga and similar slum communities all around Kampala.

———

This study, among others, set the stage for the approach we took in our collective community development work in East Africa. It was a reminder of how much more we can accomplish if we collect this kind of information in collaboration with others, instead of being an organization that flies solo and doesn't check preconceived ideas before serving a community. When you start experimenting with innovative ideas, gathering data, building empathy, and strengthening relationships with those living in the community to inform your efforts, it makes a huge difference. The Wright Brothers were innovative and transformative in their work, but before they started building a plane, they spent years on a beach in Kitty Hawk on the Outer Banks of North Carolina, just researching; they watched how birds took flight and collected prolific data based on their observations (McCullough, 2016).

On a side note, while this story is about impacting change in a hard-to-reach place like the Katanga slum community, it is also a story about community needs. Therefore, we could have placed it in the first two sections of the book to emphasize the importance of data-gathering in the listening and thinking phases of community development work. That said, gathering and interpreting data is a critical component of each aspect of the Listen. Think. Act. process and should be factored throughout community development work accordingly.

As we learned in Chapter Four, all too often outside practitioners show up in underserved communities with assumptions that are informed mainly by their biases and start implementing interventions that are misguided and uninformed. Coming to recognize that the ultimate priority for people living in the Katanga slum may actually be education doesn't change the fact that substandard housing and sanitation also need to be addressed. But it adds a layer of context and enables deeper understanding of, and empathy for, the people you are serving. You become better informed about what community members value and need. This kind of data should ultimately guide all the work that community development organizations do.

Evaluation and research can inform experimentation and move your community development in directions you had not anticipated. By uncovering information that is not always readily available on the surface, research can inspire innovation and drive lasting partnerships.

With that, we will close this chapter with a story related to communities of children born in captivity in Northern Uganda and what we learned along the way. The historical context is set around the fallout from the LRA conflict, which we started learning about in Chapter Two.

"I Have a Story to Tell," by Jamie Van Leeuwen

In the early 2000s, former abductees of the LRA began returning from the bush to the communities where they had been abducted, as the infamous Joseph Kony reportedly slipped across the border into what is now South Sudan and disappeared. What he left behind were many young people who were both victims and perpetrators of his cruel war in Northern Uganda. Victims, as they were kidnapped from their homes and forced into captivity; perpetrators, as they became instruments of terror themselves after they were trained to kill and steal.

I first met some of these young people at the Rachelle Rehabilitation Center in Lira in 2007, just as the documentary called *Invisible Children* had made a cottage industry of telling the most upsetting parts of their stories. I expected to hear similarly gruesome narratives from the youth themselves, but when I arrived in the dusty town of Lira, that was not the kind of story they wanted to tell. They wanted to talk about the struggle to return to civilian life, after inadvertently being caught up in conflict. As we came to know these young people while they were working to integrate back into their original communities, I found that I had so many questions. Most of the stories we read about this population recounted the horrors and the tragedies that child soldiers have to deal with in the bush. Not told as frequently by the media are the less intriguing or dramatic stories of what happens to these young people after they come home.

As we became acquainted with these young people, we were also working with the Cornell Institute of Public Affairs, one of our first academic partners. Every time I would visit with the youth at the Rachelle Rehabilitation Center, I would leave with the gnawing question of what we should be doing to support these young people. What did they need to succeed? What did they want? What were their intentions and their goals in life?

We could speculate that they might want to finish their schooling, which had been abruptly interrupted at the time of their abduction. They probably wanted a house and a family and a job. Perhaps they wanted health care. We made a series of broad assumptions based on what we thought we would want if we were in their situation; assumptions driven by our own cultural biases. To tease this out, we decided to listen and think with the former abductees first and find out if our speculations were correct, in partnership with graduate students from Cornell.

As usual, we learned that what we imagine would be a priority in our minds was not necessarily a priority for these young people. Housing and health care were on their list. Finishing school was a stretch, though, as many of them had been gone for years and the idea of going back to a classroom while managing the many post-traumatic stress issues that accompany experiences with conflict was a huge barrier. The age difference between the abductees and other students was quite awkward, too. Who wants to be a 24-year-old in a classroom with 17-year-olds?

Through our work with the Cornell team, we learned that what the returning abductees really wanted was job training and a way to integrate into the workforce so that they could provide for their families. They wanted economic opportunity. And so, after a year of listening and thinking with these young people, we began to explore what useful vocational skills could look like and what it would take for them to integrate into the workforce in a part of the world where employment options are quite limited (Van Leeuwen et al., 2018).

There is not a lot of industry in Lira, and service sector jobs are limited, but the local agricultural sector generates high demand for farmhands. Through our community-based research efforts, we connected with former abductees and with general community members, as well as with local NGOs who were also working with these sensitive populations. Over time, we moved from the listening and thinking phase of our research to implementation of a workforce development program involving local providers to train these youth in agricultural best practices and to assist them in moving their produce to markets.

Today we continue to innovate through experimentation, guided by the research partnership that we put in place with Cornell back in 2014. Each year, new students are engaging with local community members in Lira to ask new questions, collect data, and pose changes and adaptations to existing work. We have learned a lot along the way, but there is a lot we still have yet to learn as we continue to support the growth of these agrarian communities in Lira and to respond to the needs that children born in captivity have identified. Those young people do have an important story to tell, if we are open to listening; and that story belongs to them.

———

Summing Up

Experimentation, guided by research, can be transformative. The process of Listen. Think. Act. remains iterative, but over time, meaningful change is possible. The intention of this chapter is to show that good community development, infused with a spirit of innovation, will usually result in a robust résumé of failures. Through this process, you will define your intentions, build relationships, measure the impacts of your actions, and get better with each iteration of your listening, thinking, and acting. Ultimately, these efforts should also contribute to your résumé of successes and long-term impact in the communities where you work.

With each chapter there is a lot to unpack, but hopefully your understanding of good community development is becoming clearer. As this text progresses, you should start to see how it all ties together, from relationship building to exchanging ideas to measuring impact. Community development is complicated, and it takes time to do it well. There is so much to consider as you engage in development work; and as we have said throughout, it is an imperfect science. Even when you think you are doing it right, you will encounter biases and barriers and unforeseen situations that may lead to a course adjustment. The truly great practitioners are not those who get it right the first time, as very few people who engage in this work do; rather, the leaders who transform communities are those who are persistent. They are willing to listen and think as they implement their work, they pay attention to the results, and they adjust as needed along the way. And then they wake up the next day and do it all over again!

The truth is not in the results; they are merely indicators and road signs. The truth of good community development can be found in the process of work itself. By paying attention to the road signs, and always privileging the relationship building that constitutes the heart of the work, you can arrive where you want to go.

CHAPTER FIVE "COMMUNITY CHANGEMAKER" CHALLENGE: TEST

This next step is a big one, as you have heard from Part III of the book: take some action. Go out into the community, the real-life community that you are designing for, and connect with your user(s). Share your ideas for solutions to community challenges with your user(s) and see what they think!

- Have a phone, video, or in-person interview with your user and try to get answers to these questions:
  - What are your user's wishes for the idea and/or area of interest?
  - What is your initial reaction to your solution(s)?
  - What does your user like about your idea?
  - What does your user not like about it?
  - What would he/she/they want to see added or subtracted in the solution?
  - What other ideas do your solutions give them?
  - What else is significant from the conversation?

Our core piece of advice here... Take copious notes! Make a record of anything that seems relevant and important. As we discussed in the book, your user(s) might not always know exactly what they are looking for. Search for hidden themes or clues in people's behavior. In the final stage of your challenge, you will be iterating, prototyping, and then testing your solution again with your user(s)!

CHAPTER FIVE CONVERSATION STARTERS

We are not going to let you leave this chapter without drafting your own résumé of failures. This exercise works best if you take your time. Give this some thought over your next run or long airplane or bus ride.

- Draft your own résumé of failures and compare it to your actual résumé.
- Which is longer?
- What have you tried that did not work? This can be personal or professional.
- What do you wish you would have tried if you had not been afraid to take the risk?

Next, think about a community development issue that you have been a part of or a colleague that you know who has been a part of an initiative you are familiar with:

- What core assumptions do you hold about this issue?
- What is your role as it relates to this initiative?
- What are the roles of the other players and how are these relationships defined?
- Who is providing? Who is managing? Who is spending?
- Is there role confusion?
- How would you measure and evaluate the issue to determine if your assumptions are correct?

CHAPTER FIVE ADDITIONAL RECOMMENDED CONTENT

- Chambers, A. (2009, November 24). *Africa's not-so-magic roundabout.* The Guardian.
- Gates, B. (2017, January 9). *5 reasons I'm optimistic about Africa.* Gates-Notes.
- Gates, B., & Gates, M. (2014). *Annual Letter 2014.* Bill & Melinda Gates Foundation.
- Gates, B., & Gates, M. (2018, February 13). *10 tough questions we get asked.* GatesNotes.
- Kamadi, G., & Mugira, F. (2020, June 23). *Yala Swamp Saga: Broken Promises, Idle Land.* Pulitzer Center.
- Sachs, J. (2006). *The End of Poverty: Economic Possibilities for Our Time.* Penguin Books.
- Van Leeuwen, J. M., Sekeramayi, T., Martell, C., Feinberg, M., & Bowersox-Daly, S. (2017). *A Baseline Analysis of the Katanga Slums: Informing Urban Public Policy In Kampala, Uganda.* African Population Studies, 31(2). https://doi.org/10.11564/31-2-1057.

CHAPTER SIX
Create Lasting Impact: Transforming Communities Through Local Ownership and Sustainable Ideas

"There is immense power when a group of people with similar interests gets together to work toward the same goals."
- Idowu Koyenikan, Wealth for All: Living a Life of Success at the Edge of Your Ability (2016)

The ideal way to reach communities and assist them in their own transformation is by listening and thinking and acting… with them. That is what this book has been all about; a series of case studies, discussions, dialogues, exercises, and explanations about what it means to engage in truly good community development. This last chapter of the book is about creating a lasting impact. By this point, our hope is that you are equipped with the tools you will need to deliver meaningful impact. You know that creating a lasting impact is about listening and thinking before you act. It is about not just doing something, but standing there, and remembering always to reflect.

Your tools include techniques designed to change the governing narrative and look at topics from a different lens. Demonstrating empathy, exchanging ideas, building relationships, and innovating through experimentation all lead to community development work that can create an enduring footprint. In teaching best practices, we have tried to showcase examples of what happens when we do not follow good community development processes, and the subsequent implications. We have talked about building out your résumé of failures and the inherent challenges, biases, and misinformation we sometimes bring along with us when we arrive in a new place.

There is tension inherent in the question of whether to study healthy behaviors or deficiencies when we are trying to determine how best to respond to community issues. Should we study the contributing factors that lead to homelessness, or the practices that prevent homelessness in the first place? The true answer to this question is: it depends. It depends on what the goals of the community are and what strategies are being employed after listening and thinking with the people who live and work there. At GLI, with the advent of the COVID-19 pandemic, we are more closely seeking to understand how to prevent the virus from spreading. With our work involving HIV in East Africa, we are looking at both the factors that lead to people contracting the disease and what can be done to prevent individuals from becoming infected in the first place.

In this chapter, we assume you have mastered the skills outlined in previous pages; you know the skills that we believe lead to better outcomes, and you recognize what good community development looks like when it is being done well. Yet here is a final question for you to consider: What does it mean to create a lasting impact? Once again, for those who need an unambiguous answer, we fear that we will disappoint; there is no easy answer to this question, only shades of grey. The right answer rests in the community. What does it mean for the community to have created the kind of institutional change that will produce a lasting impact? Having watched many nonprofits operate with the intention of building a sustainable model of services, we are somewhat suspicious. We have heard many times of nonprofit executives who were sure their goal was to work themselves out of a job. But how many nonprofits have you seen work themselves out of a job by solving the issue they set out to take on?

This chapter will look at issues related to sustainability, lasting impact, and transformation and how we assess each in our efforts to create meaningful change.

What is Successful? Sustainability

According to popular definition, sustainability "is the capacity to endure in a relatively ongoing way across various domains of life" (James et al., 2015).

Sustainability, like "collaboration" or "impact", has become a popular word in community development circles. However, we cannot think of many examples that demonstrate true sustainability. How many locally based organizations have developed a revenue stream that makes them truly sustainable and able to endure over time? And if how the nonprofit has secured its existence changes, will it have the flexibility to find new sources of support and remain sustainable? For grant writing purposes, funders often want to know what efforts will be made to ensure that their investment goes toward work that will be sustainable. To which we would say, the project will be sustainable if the initial investment is used to leverage additional resources from other investors, and if the project is then able to generate revenue on its own.

Before we go further, we should define in more detail what it means to successfully achieve sustainable programs. This definition will naturally vary from project to project. However, sustainability is generally achieved after a series of partnerships and collaborations provide the resources and support to create lasting change over time, and the results generated are transformative enough to merit further reinvestment in the project, either from local or outside sources. We do not think that sustainability necessarily means that a project or organization has weaned itself off all the existing funding sources that allowed the initiative to thrive.

Let us take a deeper look at Entusi Resort and Retreat Center, in southern Uganda.

———

"Good 'Unintentional' Community Development," by: Jamie Van Leeuwen

Entusi began merely as an idea, in the early phases of listening and thinking between American and Ugandan participants in gatherings organized by the GLI. We started to bring more young people to East Africa as part of the growing academic partnerships we were establishing. Our immersion experiences were increasingly centered around Lake Bunyonyi, and we talked about finding a place where we could take the conversations we were hosting between young people and community leaders to the next level. What if we had a place of our own to embody Listen. Think. Act.? What ideas could we incubate in such a setting?

After learning of a one-acre peninsula that was owned by members of the local community, my colleagues and I started a series of conversations about what it would mean for GLI to acquire land on Lake Bunyonyi. The local family had offered to sell it to us, but we suggested that we lease it instead. We did this with the foresight that the land should really belong to local residents. I call this good "unintentional" community development: where you do the right thing without really knowing how important it is at the time! The tribal council blessed the arrangement, and we leased the land for 99 years, with an agreement culminating in a document signed by both the GLI and the land-owner. Again, our good instincts led us to insert a final clause that reads:

> "Should the GLI ever dissolve or discontinue use of the land, the [family owners] will be able to use the structures that are in place and will regain all property rights."

As we were piecing Entusi together, one toilet at a time, our local team decided that we needed to hire staff. They wanted to hire 18 staff for the center, including everyone from housekeepers to a bartender. Who needs a bartender when there is no bar, or even a place to put the bar? And what was the house-keeper going to do when we did not have any beds? We were a construction site with a couple of frames up. There was no furniture and no guests. I did not understand the suggestion at the time, but I do now.

Yet somehow, I knew to listen to the local team. On their advice, we posted the jobs, and the hiring began. We spent a week interviewing local applicants from Kabale town. It was a big deal in Kabale that there were jobs posted for a new operation called Entusi. For context, Uganda's unemployment rate in 2019 of around 13% is highly misleading, as it fails to draw critical distinctions between "formal" and "informal" employment. According to a notable eco-nomic consultancy, *Centre for Development Alternatives*, the public consensus on Uganda's true unemployment rate is closer to 83% (Walter, 2019).

Dozens of candidates showed up to apply for these Entusi positions, even though we still had no buildings in place. We still did not even have our 501(c)(3) nonprofit certification. But after that week, we had 18 staff, each commit-ting to a two-year contract. Definitely out of my comfort zone! None of the steps that I am discussing in how we built Entusi should be construed as good business decisions, or even how you should go about organizing a nonprofit project of your own. But they afforded us a lot of lessons learned along the way and reiterated the patterns of good community development that we have come to know so well throughout this book.

You see, these 18 people that we hired helped build Entusi. Motivated by the desire to have those jobs for the next two years, they were committed to making sure our dreams became a reality. They lived on-site and were part of the structure from the beginning. They were equal partners, and they felt as though they owned the project. We had 18 staff with a seat at the table. The rooms that the housekeeper now cleans are the same rooms that the housekeeper helped design and construct. The bar that our bartender now manages was built by our bartender.

As we were erecting our facility, the locals would come by in canoes to see what the hell we were building. The main building has a magnificent thatched roof that rises almost four stories high; it is a work of art and it was unbelievable to watch it being crafted by hand. As community members quietly came by in their boats for a closer look, we would invite them to come and see what our gang was up to. We learned something: the locals had never been invited to any of the other resorts around Lake Bunyonyi, which are often owned and operated by foreigners and typically cater to foreign clientele, or else rich Ugandans on holiday. Locals around the lake typically have no money to spend and therefore are rarely welcome. But we knew that our organization would thrive most easily if it occupied a place in the hearts of the locals. We were building the GLI and Entusi to connect with and serve the people in those dugout canoes. We wanted them to feel welcome and to be a part of what we were doing. We wanted them to have a seat at the table.

We started building Entusi in November of 2011. We finished most of the center in seven months —more about that later—and raised close to $300,000 in the process to fund the construction. And when I look back now, I can say that the most critical piece of all was that we did this in true partnership with the community. Relationships matter.

Almost a decade later, Entusi continues to thrive and still employs and engages with many of the people who helped us start it up. Our bartender still tends the bar, and the same housekeepers still make sure your room is ready for you when you visit. When a funder asks what sustainability looks like, we respond with Entusi. Entusi created a space for us to invite our academic partners to engage in community development conversations, launch research initiatives, and host events. Dozens of other ventures have grown out of conversations that have taken place on this campus, and it has been a site where many critical alliances have been formed, with the staff occasionally doubling as translators when needed. If you want to have a conference on best-practices community development, hosting it in a community where you are practicing community development is not a bad place to start!

Almost a decade later, Entusi generates resources from these partnerships that in turn have allowed us to continue to employ the staff and engage in the community work that we started back in 2011. It is not 100% financially independent, and we still need to generate funds to keep operating certain programs, but it has addressed a clear need for local employment opportunities and for civic dialogue. And because Entusi operates as a local private enterprise, attracting guests year-round, alongside our extensive network of academic partners, it allows us to generate ourselves much of the resources we need to sustain the work being done around the lake. You might say that it has the "capacity to endure in a relatively ongoing way" and it will continue to do so until it no longer fills those needs. And if it becomes unsustainable in the future, we have created a way for the valuable property that was created in concert with the local community to revert to local ownership.

———

But keep in mind, each successful and sustainable initiative is unique. Some enterprises last longer than others. Some efforts create change that endures for a longer period than others. Some entities grow, some stay the same size, and some go away. In thinking about this case study and the question of whether we created lasting change, we do not believe that there is a clear yes or no answer. It remains to be seen what impact Entusi will ultimately have on Lake Bunyonyi. There are many questions you can ask that will help you determine how sustainable a community development project really is, and whether the investment is working or not.

Here are three questions that we ask of every project that we consider in our community development work in Uganda:

1. Does it create employment opportunities?
2. Is it Ugandan (locally) run?
3. Does it have potential to generate revenue?

While these three questions do not ensure the sustainability of an initiative, we know that if you answer "no" to any of the above questions, then you should give some thought to whether the project you are investing in can have lasting impact.

- *Did Entusi create employment opportunities?*
  - Yes. Over 150 jobs to build it and 18 full-time jobs that are still in place 10 years later, plus much part-time work, and then some. Aside from work that has taken place directly on the campus, the retreat center has also been a location where dozens of other ventures have been hatched, and so it has also contributed to the creation of hundreds of other job opportunities in additional locations around Uganda and Rwanda.
- *Is it Ugandan (locally) run?*
  - Yes. All operations and management are handled by the local staff.
- *Does it have potential to generate revenue?*
  - Yes, but not enough. It generates enough support to leverage outside funding.
- *So ... is Entusi sustainable?*
  - We would argue yes, but it remains a work in progress. We would like to see the facility evolve to the point where it no longer requires outside funding.

With each effort you make in community development, taking the same approach to listening and thinking and constantly assessing the viability of the project will help determine how successful you become in achieving sustainability. Yet the ultimate sustainability of an initiative depends a lot on the local context as well, and the engagement of the surrounding community.

When Do You Know You Have Had an Impact?

In Chapter Five we talked about evaluating impact as a way of innovating through experimentation. But like sustainability, what does it really mean to have an impact? How can one say, with certainty, one has generated an impact on the world? In community development circles, it is generally accepted that the best way to measure impact is through "evidence-based procedures that assess the economic, social and environmental effects of public policy" (James et al., 2015).

How you determine success in the form of measurable effects will vary from one project to another, and one community to another. You could argue that the 18 people who were hired a decade ago at Entusi have contributed to the well-being of over 100 people (if you include their families) in providing a steady monthly income and access to health care benefits. Or you could say that those resources should have been used for something else and might have had a more significant impact on more people. We believe that by providing employment, we have fulfilled the greatest need that was articulated by the local community, but you might look at the situation differently. At the end of the day, how you measure impact really is up to you, the local community you serve, and the people who support the work. In the same way that Thomas wrestled with what it means to build a strong community in Chapter Two, as community development leaders, you too will need to determine how you measure success in the work you do. As we have stated throughout this book, we believe success should be defined by three pillars:

1. Did you listen to the community as you were starting your work?
2. Did you think about what it would mean to engage the community as a whole and who should have a seat at the table?
3. When you acted, how did you measure impact, and did you achieve what you set out to do?

Again, this process is iterative. As Entusi has grown over the past decade, we have cycled through this process repeatedly. In this next study, we will see how traumatic life experiences can guide and inform community development efforts to respond to the needs of a vulnerable population. While what catalyzed the listening and thinking that led to action differs, the questions we ask to assess sustainability are the same.

———

"A Lifelong Commitment to My Community," by: Agnes Igoye

At 14, armed soldiers belonging to the LRA attacked my village, and targeted me and my siblings for sexual exploitation. We managed to flee, in a treacherous journey that led us to a Catholic church. That church's yard became my home for a long time, and officially made me an Internally Displaced Person (IDP). I survived displacement, pursued education, and dedicated my life to counter human trafficking. In 20 years working to counter human trafficking, I have met trafficking survivors who have lost everything, even down to the place they called home.

Because of my own experiences, the idea of building a rehabilitation center that would serve as a shelter for survivors of human trafficking had been my longtime dream. In 2011, I made a commitment to act while at the *Clinton Global Initiative University (CGIU)*. I announced that I would build a rehabilitation center for survivors of human trafficking in Uganda that would train law enforcement and create awareness while also advocating for survivors. Besides the fear of disappointing the person to whom I made this formal commitment—former United States President Bill Clinton—I knew it was my responsibility to see this through and build a center for the sake of survivors in Uganda who needed to have a safe place to call home.

I did not wait to make a lot of money before I started, nor did I wait for development partners to fund my commitment. I just had to start, and not worry about how long it would take. While I was a student at the University of Minnesota, I utilized part of my student stipend and savings to begin the construction of the center in Uganda but lacked the funds to finish the project.

As I began serving as the Deputy National Coordinator for Prevention of Trafficking in Persons in Uganda, my determination to build the center only grew. I became increasingly frustrated by a lack of rehabilitation centers for human trafficking survivors in Uganda.

As an alternative, I opened my own house to survivors for safety. The last person to stay with me was 20 years old. At 13, she had been circumcised and forced to marry a foreign national before she healed. After years of abuse, she managed to escape to another country, in the hope of starting afresh where no one knew her. Shortly thereafter, she ran out of money and decided to go back to her parents' home. But they did not want her. They called her names and criticized her for having abandoned her marriage. They wanted her to return to her husband. When she refused, there were consequences for bringing shame to the family.

I was woken up in the middle of the night by a phone call. A frantic, traumatized voice, begging to be rescued. Her mother had beaten her, and she had managed to flee. She was grateful to have recorded my telephone number when I had shared it during one of my human trafficking awareness campaigns. Driving by myself in the middle of the night, I finally located her and took her to my house, where I lived with my mother and sister. She was grateful, but despite our attempts to make her feel at home, she felt guilty for 'intruding' into our space. Three days later, as I desperately looked for a place she could be sheltered, I returned home to find her gone. I have never seen her again. I thought about this woman constantly. If only there had been a rehabilitation center to take her! Those words kept ringing in my head, giving me the determination to finish the construction of the center for survivors, despite all the limitations I faced.

In 2016, I received the Diane von Furstenberg Award which recognizes and supports extraordinary women who are dedicated to transforming the lives of other women. I devoted the monetary proceeds to the completion of my center to rehabilitate survivors of human trafficking. We called it the "Dream Revival Center." Many survivors are lured to exploitation with the promise of a job. They often had dreams they wanted to accomplish that the exploitation suffocates. The Dream Revival Center is a place where they can be supported as they revive their lost dreams. The center provides comprehensive care, encompassing physical, psychosocial, and other health services to survivors of human trafficking in Uganda, while simultaneously leading campaigns against the crimes that were committed.

Operation of the Dream Revival Center is enabled in part by residents growing their own food on site. The center has received grants from dozens of local and international organizations, including key stakeholders like *African Women's Development Fund (AWDF)* and Vital Voices. The center has also received support for specific projects, such as when the United States Mission to Uganda funded the center's "Our Global Cultures" photo essay book, a compilation that documents Uganda as it is seen by survivors of human trafficking.

As a consistent recipient of development assistance, I can report that I have often started my most important initiatives without foreign assistance. Local ownership and long-term sustainability are always key. By the time additional supporters come on board, my colleagues and I have already figured out what problem we need to tackle and started solving it ourselves. When external support finds us prepared in this way, we feel empowered, and partnerships can become meaningful.

I have found this to be true among various community development projects: a sense of genuine ownership at the local level creates real impact. This has been the story of my life experiences.

––––––

Again, as with Entusi, we turn to our three questions to assess the sustainability of the Dream Revival Center:

1. Does it create employment opportunities?
2. Is it Ugandan (locally) run?
3. Does it have potential to generate revenue?

A strong argument can be made that all three answers are in the affirmative. As we look at how community development projects evolve to create a lasting impact, keep in mind that your efforts do not have to come in the shape of a community space or a rehabilitation center. It is also possible to build a movement. In that case, what you build and the impact that you have will be largely defined by how you generate the movement. Yet long term sustainability is still probably going to be measured through employment figures, local leadership, and revenue generation, and success still hinges on the pillars of listening, thinking, and then acting.

To understand how to build a movement, let us look at another community initiative that was born out of Entusi and assess its impact. Here we feature a community-based music festival that, over time, has become one of the largest public health initiatives in East Africa.

———

"A Ticket to the Show," by: Jamie Van Leeuwen

A young musician who joined us on one of our earliest GLI student trips was taken by the role that music played in the lives of people in Uganda. He suggested that we host a music festival on Lake Bunyonyi. We suggested that, as a budding expert in community development, he listen, think, and figure out how we might host a music festival on the lake! And that is exactly what he did. Empower young people and turn them loose and amazing things can happen. Our music festival was no exception. He returned to Tulane University where he was studying, and days later, a man by the name of Andrew Ward called to announce that he would help create our music festival. He had done a music festival in Mali already, and he was ready to branch out.

Now, some might say that Andrew is eccentric. He wears a white suit and plays banjo and has a feather hat that would make even the dancers at the Copacabana jealous. Andrew was on *America's Got Talent*, and he hosts the "Running of the Bulls" festival each year in New Orleans, an homage to Spain's famous Encierro de Pamplona, filled with roller derby skaters dressed in red horned helmets instead of real bulls.

So, Andrew assembled a group of great musicians, got them to crowd source on a shoestring budget, and brought them to Uganda. We raised a little bit more money and we put things together at the last minute, and somehow, some way, it worked. We had about 12 musicians from Denver, New Orleans, and Nashville come to Southern Uganda to jam and collaborate with local and national musicians from around Uganda. The musicians hung out on the lake, and they spent the day recording new songs and composing new music. They took "Love is My Religion" and performed it in the local language of Rukiga. The Flobots, a rap rock duo from Colorado, joined the mix and it was an extraordinary three days of sharing both culture and music. For me, that in and of itself was success. People sharing ideas and music across borders and listening and thinking rather than coming to Africa to fix things.

The plan was to host a fun, free concert for the larger community on a Saturday in Kabale town—an urban hub adjacent to Lake Bunyonyi—where we had rented out the local soccer field and could accommodate as many as 4,000 attendees. As we planned this event with the Entusi team, local health providers in Kabale and a Ugandan public health organization called Reach a Hand Uganda approached us. They requested that if we were bringing all these community members together for a concert, we should allow them to conduct HIV testing and provide some basic HIV and AIDS prevention education to the concert goers. At first, we had some hesitation; the idea seemed strange. But they explained how hard it was to get people together for an opportunity like this, and that they did not have the resources to assemble folks in the way that we were about to do. We agreed to work with them, with the caveat that the testing had to be voluntary and that anyone who tested positive needed to have access to treatment and counseling. In my mind, there was no way people in rural Uganda were going to come to a concert in droves, and even if they did, they sure as hell were not going to want to test for HIV.

Then our team designed and printed tickets to give out to the people of Kabale to attend the concert. Printing 4,000 tickets for a free concert? The idea was to put this event at no cost for entrants. Why on earth would we hand out tickets? Just let people come until there are 4,000 (if that many show), close the gates, and call it a day! But then the team sent me into town to hand out some tickets to people and see what happened. And then I got the point.

It was a big deal. My Ugandan colleagues were right, even though I did not understand that at first. People in this rural community had never been invited to attend a concert like this before. As I handed out the tickets to street-goers, I watched as each person carefully stowed them in a jacket pocket, purse, or wallet. They had a ticket to the show. They had been invited to a big event, and now they had an official seat at the table.

On the night of the show, 4,000 people did not show up to the concert. Five thousand did. On top of that, our health partners ran out of HIV tests in the first two hours; all 826 tests that they brought were administered before the music even began. And everyone who tested positive was connected to services that same night with local health care providers.

———

We would argue that this movement is what good international community development looks like; when you turn people and ideas loose, and you let them grow in their own way, you can truly be part of the transformation of a community. In terms of measuring impact, look what these music festivals GLI has been hosting have accomplished since they started in 2014:

- Over 250 artists representing Uganda, Rwanda, and the United States have performed at the concerts.
- More than 20 transnational songs have been recorded and performed.
- Over 300,000 people have attended the live concerts.
- More than 30,000 people have received a free HIV test.
- Thousands more have received additional services including screenings for various non-communicable diseases such as cervical cancer and kidney disease.
- Millions of condoms have been distributed.

Working with local health providers and in-country partners, we learned that if you bring thousands of people together for a free concert, you have a unique opportunity to provide free health services. In addition to HIV testing, the concert venues now offer free comprehensive health screenings, cervical cancer screenings, condom distribution, family planning counseling, gender-based violence prevention, reproductive health education, and mental health training.

The live music industry plays a major role in economies across the world; Uganda is no exception. Those concerts, set in rural locations, also directly invested thousands of dollars into the local economies. In 2017 alone, a GLI study estimated that the three-district iKnow Concert Series in Uganda had a combined economic impact to the tune of over $669,100—direct ($171,843) and indirect ($497,257)—or roughly the equivalent of the GDP per capita of 1,088 Ugandan people in 2016 (Ward, 2017). This impact has further grown in more recent years as the concerts have expanded their reach to Rwanda in partnership with the *Tour du Rwanda* bicycle race.

Did the music festivals have an impact and create lasting change through best practices community development?

- Did we listen to the community as we got started with the first music festival held at Lake Bunyonyi?
- Did we think about what it would mean to engage the community and who should have a seat at the table?
- When we acted, how did we measure impact and did the work achieve what we set out to do?

And in follow-up, is the music festival sustainable?

- Does it create employment opportunities?
- Is it Ugandan (locally) run?
- Does it have potential to generate revenue?

We believe you can make a strong case that the music festivals are both successful and sustainable. We would also argue that the true answer to these questions rests in the eyes of the local communities themselves but looking at the way health providers now collaborate with local community leaders in the services that are provided suggests to us that something has changed at a fundamental level. The numbers of people who will not spread HIV because of the treatment they are receiving, or the numbers of people who will not contract HIV because of the prevention services delivered, are also part of the overall impact, even though stuff that does not happen is hard to measure. And once again, as was true with each of these cases studies, we can easily identify where empathy, idea exchange, relationship building, and innovation all came into play. In fact, the music festivals would never have involved these critical health interventions if we had not chosen to collaborate with others and to listen to their ideas.

By describing our work with Entusi, the Dream Revival Center, and the many crowded music festivals we have hosted where so many people have obtained critical health interventions, our objective has been to offer case studies that use all the tools we have been providing throughout this text. Remember what we said about how to cultivate empathy, and the importance of building relationships and exchanging ideas, as well as innovation through experimentation. When you use these tools, and you start to create an Entusi, or a Dream Revival Center, or a music festival, be sure that you have gone through the process of listening and thinking and acting. Then it is imperative that you spend more time with the local community to really think about sustainability and impact. Then ultimately you decide, and act.

As we said at the beginning of this book and throughout, there are no silver bullets in community development work. We are dealing with an imperfect and complex science—one could even argue that it is more of an art—and there are no clear right answers. You could make a case for measuring both the sustainability and the true impact of all these initiatives in different ways using various metrics. But again, we believe that in the end, the truth is in the work.

Transformation

In 1964, when ruling on obscenity in *Jacobellis v. Ohio*, United States Supreme Court Justice Potter Stewart's threshold test was simple: "I know it when I see it" (Hudson Jr, 2018). We think that is the threshold test for high-impact, sustainable community development as well. To create high-impact and sustainable initiatives, you now have all the ingredients needed for transformation. But how will you know whether your work is transformative? Metrics matter. You need to gather the data, and study the figures, and keep improving what you do. But ultimately, like Justice Potter, we think you will know it when you see it.

Now there is a risk here in this general approach, as there are cases when a development organization or group thinks they know that they made a significant impact based on what they saw, but in retrospect, they were wrong. Go back to Chapter Five and add this to your résumé of failures. Ultimately, nearly anyone doing community development work believes it to be transformative. But there is a high level of subjectivity and specificity to success and impact in community development work. Perhaps a stakeholder tells you that your program has transformed their community, but in reality, the effects are not long-lasting, or the community member feels pressured to provide false affirmation about the program to satisfy the funder.

At the end of the day, community development is not only messy but is imperfect. You will make mistakes and sometimes when your work is transformative you might reassess over time. It is important to be very critical in impact assessment and engage in both qualitative and quantitative data collection to gain an unbiased view as to how the community has been affected by the program. Over time, community development work should get better and instincts as to what is truly transformative should also improve.

If you truly spend time with the community, assess the work in an ongoing and iterative way, and seek to measure the impact, you will have a good sense if what you are doing is working or not. Transformation comes when you have just the right mix of ingredients in your community development work; you have included opportunities to share stories, developed genuine empathy, exchanged ideas, built lasting relationships, and created space for innovation, while keeping in mind your résumé of failures. Mix all these ingredients together and see what happens. It will take time, and it will require a lot of listening and thinking. But when you do it right you can ignite a fire.

———

"Igniting a Fire," by: Jamie Van Leeuwen

On August 11, 2012, we formally opened up Entusi. Over the previous seven months, we had built four luxury tents and a major dorm platform to accommodate twenty guests. We had staff quarters, a storage building, two major bathroom facilities, three boat docks, and a central conference space. Entusi could now accommodate lodging for 38 guests and 10 staff. We did all of this in seven months! We built 13 buildings and created an operational retreat center in just over a half a year.

Of course, like any major project, there were moments when we tended to act more and listen and think less. I was too much in the weeds about finishing the center and activating the space to see anything outside of what remained to be done. I spent many hours dwelling on how much more money we would need to really finish Entusi. The paths weren't completed; the landscaping wasn't perfect; in many ways it still resembled a construction site. But the bones were intact. Looking back, it wasn't the building itself or the money raised to pay for the construction that represented the true accomplishment. We had done something even more extraordinary. We had engaged a community; we had ignited a fire. Sure, we created a unique and beautiful physical space. But more importantly, we had built a team, and created an oasis on the lake that would bring people together in ways that had never been done before in this community. Entusi would serve as a platform for people to start thinking differently and thinking big about how to do truly good community development work.

Although I spent many nights stressing about paint, interior lighting, and fire pits, none of that really mattered. Entusi was rooted in the community, and if we had only built one structure instead of 13, if the principles of listening and thinking before acting were in place, none of that other stuff was important. Emphasizing local ownership and buy-in, Entusi embodied the idea of giving people a seat at the table. We had worked together to create a space where everyone was welcome, and that would redefine the way we did community development in southern Uganda. On that special summer evening in August, we invited the entire community to come for our grand opening celebration. We ate local food and drank bushera (a favorite alcoholic beverage made from fermented millet and sorghum). We had over 600 people show up from around the lake, alongside a group of students and community leaders from the United States!

Folks from around the lake dressed to impress and canoed over to our peninsula. Many had never been invited to any event like this. But on this special night, they were warmly welcomed, and they all had a seat at the table as dusk fell and we celebrated the opening of Entusi. In the true spirit of a good Ugandan event, we had long speeches and a proper ceremony. We heard from the chairman, local elected officials, and our manager. We showed an inspiring video of how we built the facility, and then we dropped the screens so our guests could look out over the dark lake, where they saw that we had placed hundreds of floating candles on the water. Households all around the lake had lit fires outside their homes in response. We had ignited a fire in the community at Lake Bunyonyi; that fire was the collaboration behind the physical structures at Entusi.

And I cried. This gangly, awkward, White child of privilege, who made his first trip to Africa almost two decades before, was now a part of something incredible: a new community development journey in Uganda. When you go all-in, step outside your comfort zone, and you take on something that you are not sure is possible, there is a feeling you experience that cannot ever be explained or described. It is a feeling not of accomplishment, but of humility and joy; knowing that you were a small but important part of what happened. You too had a seat at the table. It is a feeling of knowing that what happened was possible because you invited hundreds of others to share their ideas, and that through this continued exchange, your own ideas changed over time, but the core values of Listen. Think. Act. remained intact.

As the guests kept arriving in larger numbers, we did not realize over the course of the evening, as folks ate and danced and sang, that not every person left on the boat in which they arrived. At about two in the morning, we had way too many people and not enough boats! But in the true spirit of good community development, like everything else we had done to this point, we figured it out. We hired more boats, and by 4 a.m. we had turned the music off, the DJ went home, and Entusi went to sleep. But only for a couple of hours. Our work here had just begun. What I did not realize at the time of the grand opening was that a new chapter in the ongoing story of learning how to do community development in the right way was just beginning. To build the physical retreat center was one thing; to activate it was quite another. Arguably the most important impact to come from Entusi has been all of the HIV testing, treatment, and other health care interventions we have provided to the thousands of people who have flocked to our music festivals, but back then I had no idea that the retreat center would become the key place where visiting musicians and local musicians would swap songs and ideas in a freeform way that would somehow result in that innovative collaboration with health care providers which would touch so many lives. I just sensed that a magical kind of fire had been lit, and that it would grow.

These are some stories of transformation. While there is no exact way to measure certain kinds of success, we believe that the three pillars of listening, thinking, and acting can provide a stable foundation for your initiatives. At the same time, local leadership coupled with employment and revenue creation speak to the overall sustainability of initiatives. But you will know true collaboration when you see it. People who built Entusi knew it the night that the rest of the community lit the fires in front of their homes all around the lake; the founder of the Dream Revival Center knew it on the first night that a young woman stayed at the center; the creators of the music festivals knew it when the American and Ugandan musicians walked onto a stage with 5,000 cheering fans at their initial show. You will know it when you put the basic tools described in this book to work and set out to light your own fire.

Let the skills, ideas, and stories you find in this book guide you on your next journey. Embrace the art and science of good community development, work with others to light your own fire, and fan the flames as you work together in partnership to make the world a better, more equitable place.

CHAPTER SIX "COMMUNITY CHANGEMAKER" CHALLENGE: ITERATE, PROTOTYPE, TEST

This final stage is arguably one of the most important stages of your challenge! You have shared and tested some of your ideas with your user(s), so now:
- Iterate. Develop the idea further. Work to transform your idea from words on a page to something more tangible. What would this look like

if implemented? Depending on your idea, you may need to draw it on a piece of paper or make a diagram with labels.

- Prototype. Bring your idea to life. Create a physical version of your idea, something that your user(s) can genuinely interact with. If your idea is a large-scale systematic change, then break it down. Are there specific steps that you can create a simpler version of?
- Use whatever you can find, the key here is to create a model that can be genuinely interacted with.
- Test again. Go back out into your community and engage with more users. Follow similar guidance from the "test" stage in Chapter Five. But this time, have your user engage with your idea. Try to find a way for your user(s) to engage with a representation of your ideas, rather than you simply telling them. This is why it's so important to make something physical and tangible.
  - For this final stage, try using the "feedback capture grid template" from *Design Thinking Playbook*'s website (Design Thinking Playbook, 2021). This will help you answer questions like:
    - What worked about your idea?
    - What might you need to improve about your idea?
    - What questions came up from your user?
    - Any new problems you had not considered before?
    - Any other ideas that have arisen from your testing experience?

You are now about to reach the finish line… sort of! While you have journeyed through one version of the design thinking process, do not think you are done forever. An inherent quality to human-centered design is that it's iterative and constantly changing, just like communities. You will need to go back to various stages of the process again, and do not be discouraged. You are not done forever, but you are making progress, and learning a lot along the way!

CHAPTER SIX CONVERSATION STARTERS

We are giving you three different questions, each requiring you to come up with a unique example! These can be projects/initiatives that you were directly involved with, or something you have researched/heard about.

- Think about a real-world project that you would describe as sustainable and make your case for why that is so.
- Think about a project that is impactful and make your case as to why it has real results.

- And finally, think about a project that is transformative. Is it also sustainable and high impact? Make your case one last time around about how you know it is transformative.
- One extra question, do these three attributes apply in tandem or independent from one another? In other words, if a community development project is high impact, does that mean it's also sustainable and transformative, or not necessarily?
- Mix and match the terms and discuss using real-world examples.

CHAPTER SIX ADDITIONAL RECOMMENDED CONTENT

- Adams, J., Niringiyimana, J., Van Leeuwen, J. M., Ward, A., Gumbie, R., & Karrel, T. (2019). *Music as a vehicle for reducing HIV stigma and increasing access to testing in rural Uganda: A quasi-experimental, mixed-methods study.* Sociology International Journal, 3(6). https://doi.org/10.15406/sij.2019.03.00208.
- Gelaro, B., Amanya, J., Whitten, M. S., Van Leeuwen, J., Lindstrom, M., Karrel, T., & Pinckney, J. (2019). *Down Syndrome in Uganda: Identifying Barriers and Making Recommendations to Increase Access.* International Journal of Social Sciences and Management Review, 2(4).
- Lupton, R. D. (2016). *Charity Detox: What Charity Would Look Like If We Cared About Results.* HarperOne.
- Sachs, J. D., & Ki-Moon, B. (2015). *The Age of Sustainable Development* (Illustrated ed.). Columbia University Press.
- Sternin, J., & Choo, R. (2000, February). *The Power of Positive Deviancy.* Harvard Business Review (Magazine).
- Vanderwerken, M., Amanya, J., Fullenbach, E., Herman, K., Karrel, T., Tesconi, W., Van Leeuwen, J. (2019). *Introducing Electricity and Renewable Energy Platforms in Rural Uganda: A Case Study on Lake Bunyonyi.* International Journal of Social Sciences and Management Review, 2(1).
- Van Leeuwen, J., Nabimanya, H., Ward, A., Grundy, R., & Thrun, M. (2018). *Music Festivals Serving as a Catalyst for Collaborative HIV Prevention Education and Expanded HIV Testing in Rural Uganda.* International Journal of Community Development, 6(1), 1. https://doi.org/10.11634/233028791503915.
- Van Leeuwen, J., & Feinberg, M. (2018, March). *Impact Investing in Africa: A Case Study on East Africa.* Wilson Center (Africa Program).
- Van Leeuwen, J., Adkins, S., Mirassou-Wolf, T., Schweiger, W. K., & Grundy, R. (2016). *An evaluation of the Mental Health Facilitator programme in rural Uganda: Successes and recommendations for future implementation.* Journal of Psychology in Africa, 26(3), 288–299. https://doi.org/10.1080/14330237.2016.1185919.

EPILOGUE
TUGENDE

"They say a journey of a thousand miles begins with a single step. I took mine and fell flat on my face. As a young woman, I dreamed of changing the world. In my twenties, I went to Africa to try and save the continent, only to learn that Africans neither wanted nor needed saving. Indeed, when I was there, I saw some of the worst that good intentions, traditional charity, and aid can produce... I concluded that if I could only nudge the world a little bit, maybe that would be enough. But nudging isn't enough."
- Jacqueline Novogratz, The Blue Sweater: Bridging the Gap Between Rich and Poor in an Interconnected World

In Central Uganda's native language of Luganda, "tugende" means "we go." Our epilogue is about this: "where do we go from here?"

This book is our comprehensive take on what it means to do good community development work. We have shared lots of stories, reflections, observations, and experiences guided by the core values of Listen. Think. Act. Our hope is that you realize that there really is no one cookbook or secret ingredient to doing good community development. Like we did, you must go and make your own stories and figure out how to put them all together with your own secret sauce. You need to have your own lightning bolt moments and build your own Entusi or your own Dream Revival Center that will no doubt challenge the way that you think about the world, pushing you to listen and think and act in ways you never dreamed of doing before.

In this respect, the people who read this book are community development artists-in-training. Like the three people who wrote this, you are on a journey of discovery that does not end. All three of us are still learning through this same type of iterative process and if we rewrite this book in five years or ten years it will most likely be a different read.

We wrote this book to share what we believe is the best way possible to do community development work. Tomorrow, or five years from now, we will know even more, and we expect that our community development outlook will shift to be slightly different. We talked about the extraordinary lessons we have accumulated along the way, from slews of mentors, colleagues, friends, and family who have been a part of the journeys that each of us have taken. Journeys where we have wrestled with how to get a homeless kid off the streets and into housing, where our own notions of what constitutes strong communities were transformed, and where we have engaged with communities on ways to reinvent their lives after experiencing extraordinarily tough and often traumatic circumstances. Journeys that required us to change the narratives we held about the world and to reach deep to build empathy on issues that were outside of our comfort zone. Exchanging ideas, building relationships, innovating through experience, and creating impact in a collaborative fashion are all part of this community development journey. And as with the journeys you will take, we started without always knowing how we would get to where we wound up. But we developed confidence that if we listen and we think before we act, we tend to arrive at our destination. At least most of the time. Because even when you listen and think, you still screw up from time to time, and need to adjust. That is what community development should be about. Learning as we go, and when we do it wrong, working in partnership with the local community to do it better and to make it right—to change the way we use the boat!

We wanted this book to inspire others to believe we all have a role to play in solving complex social issues. We wanted to impart critical advice about the need for listening and thinking before we act, and to encourage others to think differently and think bigger about the approach we take in our attempt to improve the lives of people living in various communities around the world. We believe that in the future, the private sector will play a critical role in moving people out of poverty in the next decade through jobs, skills training, and workforce development. We believe that many members of the NGO community can fall into behaving like the neo-colonialists of the 21st century, and we think they should be called out when they do this. Many times, NGOs and their leaders are looking for the "quick fix" to complex issues, and we know that any given trend, be it micro-financing or social impact bonds or impact investing, while highly effective in targeted communities, is not the silver bullet to solving poverty everywhere. With over six decades of community development work among the three of us, we do not believe there is one quick fix. We do believe that successes can be achieved through a blend of innovative collaboration and strategic interventions where everyone has a seat at the table and there is local ownership of initiatives. And this kind of approach simply takes significant time.

We also wanted this book to be about stories. Stories that we hope share the lessons that have informed our work and helped us do better in communities located in all corners of the world. Stories that make you laugh; stories that make you cry; and stories that piss you off. These stories, and the ones that you will gather on your journeys, teach valuable lessons. They feed the soul, and they take all that we learn in the world and bring that wisdom into the classroom. They help to make policy better informed by practice.

That said, we also believe that modern societies tend to over complicate or dramatize complex social issues, and that many of those problems are more solvable than people are led to believe. For example, homelessness is without question ultimately solvable. If you want fewer homeless people, then house them. Connect them with support services, put a roof over their heads, and as we learned, make sure they have a playground! If you want fewer poor people in Uganda, then give them a decent paying job; connect them with the private, public, and non-governmental sectors, and employ them.

Having given this book a lot of thought and spent many hours laboring to write this all down, the pages you have read are a combination of all our best-practice conversations, and the things that we know work from experience. We hope that by sharing stories and perspectives from the field, you can learn more about good community development than you would from any technical textbook. We hope that this approach to best practices will even rattle some cages and create some discomfort in the status quo, as we believe the nonprofit community needs a nudge.

Philanthropy is changing, and in many cases, it is getting smarter. In a world of finite resources, those who think differently and collaborate across sectors through relationships, ideas, empathy, and innovation, will become the game changers. Collaboration and leveraging partnerships are the keys to delivering results, and measuring impact is critical, but do not forget to find joy in the work. Through smarter community development, our field can, and should, do better. We should be having these kinds of blunt and honest conversations across national and international boundaries. We should not be afraid to push back with one another and position a critical eye to the approaches we have taken in the past to serving the poor. We should always try to listen more, think more, and then act; when we act, we should look for impact, and measure what truly works.

At the same time, like Merton, we urge you not to depend on the hope of results, but rather on the value, the rightness, and the truth of the work itself. At the end of the day, it is the value of personal relationships that saves everything. This is what always lies at the heart of good community development work, and it is with relationships where we will end.

We know everyone reading this book has areas of interest, and plenty of ideas on how to improve the life and vitality of those in their own respective communities. Do not hold yourself back from community development work simply because others have failed, and it feels daunting. You will be surprised what you can accomplish when you lead with an attitude of genuine interest, empathy, and curiosity. And finally, please do not forget the human side of community development work. Whether you become a thriving investment banker, a hotel tycoon, a first-grade teacher, or an accomplished welder, never lose sight of the people you are serving. It is easy to get lost in the outcomes and the measurable goals we set for our organizations. There are great ways to assess and evaluate impact and ensure that there is measurable evidence of moving the needle. Always remember there is a human being that you serve whom you should never forget whether you are doing work in the United States or Uganda. Do not forget to make sure your playground is within walking distance!

That is what good community development is all about. It is about taking all the things we have talked about and integrating them into the work you do, but most importantly, it is about not ever forgetting the value of the people you serve.

So, take your first step. Reinvent the narrative, build empathy, exchange ideas, forge strong relationships, innovate through experimentation, and create lasting impact for people in your community.

Listen. Think. Act.

ACKNOWLEDGEMENTS

Since the inception of the Global Livingston Institute, there is really no one person who can take credit for what has been created by adhering to the core values of Listen. Think. Act. When you listen, think, and act as a consistent, iterative process, the resulting change in communities should improve over time, and there is a lot more to learn along the way. Looking back on the past 12 years of our collective work in East Africa, there are so many people that taught us about how to effectively engage and empower communities. All these ideas, experiences, perspectives, and teachings are packed into this book, and if we thanked everyone for what they contributed to this text, it would require a separate book.

That said, there are some specific people that we want to recognize, who have really helped us condense all this information into a text that we hope will contribute to doing better community development around the world.

The GLI built its successes on the ideas and insights of inspiring young leaders who join our team to build their experience in the international development arena, and to grow in their capacity to impact positive change. One of those innovators is Lily DeMuth, a "Jane of all trades" who has helped us assemble this book since its inception. Helen Thorpe agreed to serve as our editor after traveling with us to Uganda in 2016 to inform her own work on refugees. The insight and perspective that Helen brings to her writing truly humanizes the people she encounters, and we could think of no better person to guide this text.

There were other fearless proofreaders and pundits who provided us with invaluable insights and feedback on this book. They include JoAnn Beaupre, Wendy Bolyard, Nathan Davis, Angela Thieman Dino, Ryan Grundy, John Karrel, Denis Kibirige, Andrew Ward, and Cheryl Zimlich. These people have served as wise guides to our work, and for their commitment to this book we are truly grateful.

Thanks to Steve Sander, who, during a run around Kigali, Rwanda almost a decade ago, came up with the idea for GLI's motto of "Listen. Think. Act." And thanks to Paul Teske and the University of Colorado Denver School of Public Affairs, where we launched our first academic partnership for the GLI. They had the vision to think different and big about what a truly global classroom could look like.

Special thanks to our entire GLI community who provided quotes, stories, and experiences that fuel the content of this book, along with literally hundreds of community partners and leaders who have shaped the work we have done over the years, and subsequently this text.

Finally, we would like to thank our families and friends who endure those of us who have been bitten by the community development bug. Listening, thinking, and acting takes a lot of time and can be all-consuming to truly transform the communities where we work. There are many people in our lives who believe in this work because they believe in us, and without them this work would not be possible.

As authors there is something quite humbling about writing the acknowledgements section of your own book. This work that we are putting forward honestly has only a tiny fraction to do with the three of us. Thank you to every single person connected with GLI, who over the past 12 years, have stood steadfast with us to Listen. Think. Act.

ABOUT THE AUTHORS

Agnes Igoye serves as the Deputy National Coordinator in Uganda for the Prevention of Trafficking in Persons and is the Commandant of the Uganda Immigration Training Academy. She is also a commitment mentor at Clinton Global Initiative University, a senior New Voices Fellow at Aspen Institute, and serves on several nonprofit boards. She holds a master's degree in Sociology from Makerere University, a mid-career master's degree in Public Administration from the Harvard Kennedy School, a certificate from Oxford University, and was a Humphrey Fellow of Public Policy at the University of Minnesota. When she is not travelling to different corners of the world to share her wisdom, Agnes lives in Kampala, Uganda.

Thomas Karrel is Director of Academic Partnerships for the Global Livingston Institute, and has worked with several international development organizations over the past five years. His current professional focus is designing cross-cultural, experiential student learning programs aimed at teaching the principles of community development and runs GLI's "Global Classroom". Thomas graduated from Tulane University with a master's degree in Public Health and has lived in Uganda for over four years. He still makes time each year to visit his family and friends in the United States and is an avid tennis player and lover of yoga and meditation practice.

Jamie Van Leeuwen wears many hats, but primarily serves as CEO and Founder of the Global Livingston Institute and Director of Youth and Community Engagement with Emerson Collective. Prior to these roles, he served under both Mayor and Governor John Hickenlooper for 14 years as a public sector leader in Denver, Colorado. Through his work in local and state politics, he has engaged collectively across sectors to generate over $300 million in new resources for the public good. Jamie has a PhD in Public Policy from the University of Colorado Denver, and dual master's degrees in Public Health and Sociology from Tulane University. He is an inaugural Livingston Fellow and a Fulbright Scholar. He works as Adjunct Faculty at the University of Colorado Denver and Lingnan University in Hong Kong. Jamie presently splits his time between Denver, Colorado, Washington, D.C. and wherever his husband Andrei is based.

REFERENCES

PROLOGUE

Phyllis M. Taylor Center for Social Innovation and Design Thinking. (2021, April). *Design Thinking for Social Innovation.*

IDEO. (2021). *Foundations in Design Thinking Certificate.* IDEO U.

Raz, A. (2018, February 7). *Get Started with Design Thinking.* Stanford d.School.

CHAPTER ONE

Amin, J. A. (2016, September 19). *America's legendary ignorance about Africa persists.* The Conversation.

Baldé, C. P., Forti, V., Gray, V., Kuehr, R., & Stegmann, P. (2017). *The Global E-waste Monitor 2017.* United Nations University (UNU), International Telecommunication Union (ITU) & International Solid Waste Association (ISWA).

Custers, R., & Matthysen, K. (2009, August). *Africa's natural resources in a global context* (Antwerp). IPIS.

Dam, R. F., & Siang, T. Y. (2021, January 2). *5 Stages in the Design Thinking Process.* The Interaction Design Foundation.

Desjardins, J. (2020, February 19). *Mapped: Visualizing the True Size of Africa.* Visual Capitalist.

Farmer, P., & Weigel, J. (2013). *To repair the world: Paul Farmer speaks to the next generation (dissertation).* University of California, Berkeley Press.

Gladwell, M. (2006, February 13). *Million-Dollar Murray: Why problems like homelessness may be easier to solve than to manage.* The New Yorker.

Herbst, J. (2014). *States and Power in Africa: Comparative Lessons in Authority and Control* - Second Edition (Princeton Studies in International History and Politics, 149) (2nd ed.). Princeton University Press.

Gallup. (2019). U.S. *Adult's Knowledge About the World.* Council on Foreign Relations.

Hadithi Africa. (2020, February 10). *Here's what you need to know about the 3000 tribes in Africa.* | Hadithi Africa. Hadithi Africa | A Platform for the African Narrative.

HUD (Department of Housing & Urban Development). (2018, December). *2018 AHAR: Part 1 - PIT Estimates of Homelessness in the*

U.S. HUD Exchange.

Illich, I. (1968, April 20). *To Hell with Good Intentions*. Conference on InterAmerican Student Projects (CIASP); University of Vermont.

Kermeliotis, T., & Veselinovic, M. (2014, June 10). *The numbers that show Africa is buzzing with entrepreneurial spirit.* CNN.

Kubania, J. (2015, July 6). *How second-hand clothing donations are creating a dilemma for Kenya.* The Guardian.

Kästle, K. (2021). *Spoken languages of African countries.* One World Nations Online.

Forum on China-Africa Cooperation. (2009, October 12). *Languages of Africa.* Ministry of Foreign Affairs, the People's Republic of China.

National Alliance to End Homelessness. (2021). *State of Homelessness: 2021 Edition.*

Nursing@USC Blog. (2021, June 24). *Unsafe and Unwell: How Homelessness Affects Women and How to Help - Nursing@USC.*

Signé, L. (2019, April 3). *Africa's emerging economies to take the lead in consumer market growth.* The Brookings Institution.

UNDP. (2011, October). *Valuing Volunteering In Africa.* UN Volunteers. Conference presentation by the United Nations Volunteers Programme (UNDP); Mombasa, Kenya.

Vickers, G. (1977). *The weakness of western culture.* Futures, 9(6), 457–473. https://doi.org/10.1016/0016-3287(77)90076-3.

Vitali, A., Hunt, K., Jackson, H., Thorp, F., V., Williams, A., & The Associated Press. (2018, December 14). *Trump referred to Haiti and African nations as "shithole" countries.* NBC News.

CHAPTER TWO

Adichie, C. N. (2009, October 7). *The danger of a single story.* TED Talks.

Boyle, G. (2019, January 25). *One of The Most Inspirational Speeches From Gangsters | Father Gregory Boyle.* Pepperdine University Keynote Address. YouTube.

Bunting, I. (2017, August 24). *Lord's Resistance Army | rebel organization.* Encyclopedia Britannica.

Cavanagh, T. (2005). *Constructing ethnographic relationships: Reflections on key issues and struggles in the field.* Waikato Journal of Education, 11, 27-41.

Ditkowsky, A. (2020, December 23). *How to Build Empathy and Strengthen Your School Community.* Making Caring Common.

Hacker, R. (2018, February 21). *Six steps to improve your emotional intelligence | Ramona Hacker | TEDxTUM.* TED Talks.

Hardee, J. (2003). *An Overview of Empathy.* The Permanente Journal. Published. 7(4): 51–54. https://doi.org/10.7812/tpp/03-072.

Kelly, T. (2018, November 7). *Build Your Creative Confidence: Empathy Maps.* IDEO.

Murphy, A. (2021, February 12). *How to Be More Empathetic: 5 Ways to Build Empathy.* Declutter The Mind.

Myers, V. (2014, December 15). *How to overcome our biases? Walk boldly toward them.* TED Talks.

Revesz, R. (2017, September 26). *Former neo-Nazi has swastika tattoo removed after befriending black police officer.* The Independent.

Sherwood, J. (2017). *What is cultural competence?* The University of Sydney.

SkillsYouNeed. (2021). *Understanding Other People.* SkillsYouNeed.

UNDP. (2021). Human Development Index (HDI) | Human Development Reports. United Nations Development Programme.

University of California Berkeley School of Law. (2009). *The Prevention of Trafficking In Persons Act.* Uganda Printing and Publishing Corporation (UPPC).

CHAPTER THREE

Ayres, E. (2000). *God's Last Offer: Negotiating for a Sustainable Future.* Four Walls Eight Windows. Pg 195.

Belle, N., & Cantarelli, P. (2017b). *What Causes Unethical Behavior? A Meta-Analysis to Set an Agenda for Public Administration Research.* Public Administration Review, 77(3), 327–339. https://doi.org/10.1111/puar.12714.

Brien, S. (2020, February 7). *The Africa Prosperity Report 2019–2020.* Legatum Institute.

Day, J. L. (2019, March 25). *Lee Roper-Batker Announces Retirement After 18 Years as President & CEO of the Women's Foundation of Minnesota.* Women's Foundation of Minnesota.

EPA. (2016, October 6). *Climate Impacts on Agriculture and Food Supply.* United States Environmental Protection Agency.

National Research Council. (1992). *Democratization in Africa: African Views, African Voices.* Washington, DC: The National Academies Press. https://doi.org/10.17226/2041.

Hubert H. Humphrey School of Public Affairs. (2015). *Dennis Donovan.* University of Minnesota.

Hubert H. Humphrey School of Public Affairs. (2015). *Harry Boyte.* University of Minnesota.

Forliti, A. (2011, February 7). *Somali gangs move into sex trafficking, fraud.*

NBC News.

Gates, B., & Gates, M. (2014). *Annual Letter 2014*. Bill & Melinda Gates Foundation.

Giovetti, O. (2020, September 17). *The world's 10 poorest countries*. Concern Worldwide US.

Howard, P. N., Duffy, A., Freelon, D., Hussain, M. M., Mari, W., & Mazaid, M. (2011). Opening Closed Regimes: What Was the Role of Social Media During the Arab Spring? SSRN Electronic Journal. https://doi.org/10.2139/ssrn.2595096.

Johnso, B. (2020, July 17). Idea Exchange. On Course College Educator Workshops & Conferences.

Klein, N. (2015). *This Changes Everything: Capitalism vs. The Climate*. Simon & Schuster.

Leonard, D., & Rayport, J. (2014, August 1). *Spark Innovation Through Empathic Design*. Harvard Business Review.

McBride, J. (2018, October 1). *How Does the U.S. Spend Its Foreign Aid?* Council on Foreign Relations.

McKenna, P. (2020, December 7). *Climate Change Worsened Global Inequality, Study Finds*. Inside Climate News.

Muroyama, J. H., & Guyford, H. (1988). *Globalization of Technology: International Perspectives*. National Academies Press. https://doi.org/10.17226/1101.

Myers, S. L., Wu, J., & Fu, C. (2020, January 17). *China's Looming Crisis: A Shrinking Population*. The New York Times.

Newey, S. (2019, April 7). *From horror to health: How Rwanda rebuilt itself to become one of Africa's brightest stars*. The Telegraph.

Nkrumah, K. (2009). *Neo-Colonialism: The Last Stage of Imperialism*. Panaf.

Nnamdi, U. (2016, January 15). *Navigating Nkrumah's Theory of Neo-colonialism in the 21st Century*. E-International Relations.

Ream, M. (2019, February 12). *Kenya: Africa's innovation hub*. ShareAmerica.

Shapshak, T. (2018, December 28). *Following Mobile Money's Rise In Africa, Mobile Banking Is Now* Booming. Forbes.

Signé, L., & Gurib-Fakim, A. (2019, January 25). *Africa is an opportunity for the world: Overlooked progress in governance and human development*. The Brookings Institution.

The Associated Press. (2009, June 10). *Mystery surrounds death of Somali teen*. NBC News.

The Global Programs and Strategy Alliance. (2018, September 26). *Distinguished Leadership Award for Internationals (Agnes Igoye) | 2014*

Recipients. University of Minnesota.

World Bank. (2021). *Mali | Data*. World Bank Group.

World Bank. (2021). *Uganda | Data*. World Bank Group.

CHAPTER FOUR

Cambridge Dictionary. (2021, July 21). *'Collaboration' Definition*. Cambridge Dictionary Online.

Herbst, J. (2014). *States and Power in Africa: Comparative Lessons in Authority and Control - Second Edition (Princeton Studies in International History and Politics, 149)* (2nd ed.). Princeton University Press.

Merton, T. (1966, February 21). *Letter To A Young Activist*. Historic Reflections.

Osseiran, N. (2019, June 18). *1 in 3 people globally do not have access to safe drinking water – UNICEF, WHO*. World Health Organization.

Reeb, R. (2021, March 10). *Thinking It Through: Defending the nation of (and with) free speech*. Victorville Daily Press.

The Cultural Landscape Foundation. (2020). *Skyline Park*. The Cultural Landscape Foundation.

Williams, M. (2019, November 8). *Why I'll Never Go on a Mission Trip Again - ZORA*. Medium.

Younis, B. M. (2021, March 23). *Americans Want More, Not Less, Immigration for First Time*. Gallup.

CHAPTER FIVE

BBC News. (2017, April 13). *The Ugandan children who canoe to school*. BBC News (Africa).

Cambridge University Press. (2021). *'Community Development' Definition*. Cambridge Business English Dictionary.

Covey, S. R. (2021). *The 7 Habits of Highly Effective People: Powerful Lessons in Personal Change*. Turtleback Books; Reprint edition (2013–11-19).

Dalrymple, S., & Smith, K. (2015, June). *Coordinating Decision-Making: Meeting Needs | Mapping donor preferences in humanitarian response*. Global Humanitarian Assistance: A Development Initiative.

Gningui, C. (2020, February 13). *Uganda: Bunyonyi, A Lake of History*. AfricaNews.

Grün, G. C. (2020, December 5). *COVID-19 Vaccinations: What's the Progress?* Deutsche Welle.

Gumbie, R. A., & Van Leeuwen, J. (2021). A Call for a More Efficient Platform for Funding and Advocacy in International Development. *Public Integrity, 23*(4), 451–454. https://doi.org/10.1080/1 0999922.2021.1918419.

Iacocca, L., & Novak, W. (1986). *Iacocca: An Autobiography* (1st paperback ed.). Bantam

McCullough, D. (2016). *The Wright Brothers* (Reprint ed.). Simon & Schuster

OECD. (2006). *Recent Trends in Official Development Assistance to Health.* Organization for Economic Co-Operation and Development.

PeerNetBC. (2020, October 16). *About Us.* PeerNetBC.

Van Leeuwen, J. M., Sekeramayi, T., Martell, C., Feinberg, M., & Bowersox-Daly, S. (2017). *A Baseline Analysis of the Katanga Slums: Informing Urban Public Policy in Kampala, Uganda.* African Population Studies, 31(2). https://doi.org/10.11564/31-2-1057.

Van Leeuwen, J., Miller, L., Amanya, J., & Feinberg, M. (2018, March). *Forced to Fight: An Integrated Approach to Former Child Soldiers in Northern Uganda.* Wilson Center (Africa Program).

CHAPTER SIX

Bokua, R. (2020). *Entusi Resort & Retreat Center.* Entusi Resort & Retreat Center Website.

Design Thinking Playbook. (2021). *Feedback-Capture-Grid | Design Thinking.* Design Thinking Playbook.

Walter, M. (2019, May 22). *Why Everyone is Wrong About Youth Unemployment in Uganda.* Hire the Youth.

Ward, A. (2017, September 22). *Economic Impact of the HIV Awareness "iKnow" Concert Series on the Local Economies of Lira, Masaka, & Kabale, Uganda.* Report Prepared by Global Livingston Institute (GLI).

Hudson Jr., D. L. (2018b). *Jacobellis v. Ohio.* The First Amendment Encyclopedia.

James, P. (2014). *Urban Sustainability in Theory and Practice: Circles of sustainability (Advances in Urban Sustainability)* (1st ed.). Routledge.

EPILOGUE

Novogratz, J. (2009). *The Blue Sweater: Bridging the Gap Between Rich and Poor in an Interconnected World* (1st ed.). Rodale Books.

BACK COVER PHOTO DESCRIPTION

As the world was adapting to a new normal, so was the Global Livingston Institute. The GLI's 2020 virtual youth summit showed us all that we do not have to be in the same room to change the world collectively. The 2020 participants were made up of youth leaders from Uganda, Rwanda, and the United States, who translated GLI's motto of "Listen. Think. Act" into art, inspiring this mural.

Ugandan artist Sparrow (Founder of Afri-cans, a Kampala-based street arts festival) led students through an interactive workshop to brainstorm a design that embodies Listen. Think. Act. for a mural that he and his team (Hussein Fatumah, Phillip Rachkara, and Ian Nny-anzi) brought to life in August 2020 at Kabale Main Stadium, Kabale, Uganda. This book's cover is a photo of that mural and a reminder that good community development happens when we Listen. Think. Act.

Want to learn more?

Go to https://www.globallivingston.org/ to see how GLI works to Listen. Think. Act. with communities around the world.

Ingram Content Group UK Ltd.
Milton Keynes UK
UKHW041551090523
421401UK00027B/341